Unorthodox Encounters

Books by Uri Geller

Change Your Life in One Day, Marshall Cavendish, 1990
Dead Cold, Headline Feature, 1999
Ella, Headline Feature, 1998
Mind Medicine, Element, Chrysalis Books/Barnes and Noble, 1999
My Story, Praeger/Robson/Warner, 1975
Shawn, GoodyerAssociates, 1990
The Geller Effect, Henry Holt/Jonathan Cape/Grafton, 1998
Uri Geller's Little Book of Mind Power, Robson, 1998
Uri Geller's Fortune Secrets, Sphere, 1987
Uri Geller's Mind-Power Kit, Penguin/Virgin, 1996
Uri Geller's ParaScience Pack, van de Meer, 2000
Chippy's Magic Cadillac, Marshall Cavendish, 2002
Confessions of a Psychic and a Rabbi, Robson/Source, 2001
Life Signs, Reader's Digest, 2002

Books about Uri Geller

The Amazing Uri Geller, Martin Ebon, New American Library
The Geller Papers, Charles Panati, Houghton Mifflin
The Geller Phenomenon, Colin Wilson, Aldus Books
In Search of Superman, John Wilhelm, Pocket Books
The Metal Benders, John Hasted, Routledge
The Strange Story of Uri Geller, Jim Colin
Superminds, John G. Taylor, Picador
Uri, Andrya Puharich, Doubleday

Most of Uri Geller's books, columns and lots of other fascinating
information and pictures, relating to him and his work, including
his biography, are available on his website: www.urigeller.com
You can also email Uri Geller at urigeller@compuserve.com

Unorthodox Encounters

Uri Geller

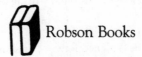 Robson Books

First published in Great Britain in 2001 by Robson Books,
64 Brewery Road, London N7 9NY

A member of the Chrysalis Group plc

British Library Cataloguing in Publication Data
A catalogue record for this title is available from the British Library.

ISBN 1 86105 366 5

Typeset by FiSH Books, London WC1
Printed in Great Britain by Butler & Tanner Ltd., London and Frome

Contents

Acknowledgements

I would like to thank Paul Harris, editor of the *Jewish Telegraph*, who has given me a regular platform to voice my opinions, no matter how controversial or way-out these may have seemed to his readers at the time. Also Chris Stevens, always on hand with good editorial suggestions when I travel, and my editor Natalie at Robson Books.

Finally my thanks go to my friend and publisher Jeremy Robson and to his wife Carole, who published my auto-biography nearly thirty years ago, and have remained close family friends ever since.

Introduction

Some instants of our lives are relived a thousand times. The happy bewildered smiles on my face and Hanna's on our wedding day; the joy when I first held my children, Daniel and Natalie; the laughter when my mother threw a ball to me in the street outside our Tel Aviv apartment. All these moments were captured on camera, and are framed on the walls of our home, and I experience them anew every day of my life.

Other moments are replayed at a TV producer's whim, when glimpses of my appearances as a spoonbender in the Seventies are repeated on compilation broadcasts. I watch myself gently stroking the stalk of metal and giggling excitedly as the bowl suddenly droops and drops off, to the incomprehension of David Dimbleby or – my own favourite – the gibbering amazement of John Noakes on *Blue Peter*. And I have watched, far too many times, the night on Johnny Carson's show when my powers drained away in the face of an onslaught of negativity, and an audience across America wondered what all the fuss was supposed to be about.

But most moments of life are fleeting, and when they are gone they cannot be recaptured and are forgotten. I am a passionate man, and I hold my opinions strongly. I give voice to them loudly and, if you argue with me, I will argue back fiercely. Then the moment passes, and I become passionate about something else, and I forget whatever it was that possessed me so strongly for those few minutes.

After I completed my novel *Ella*, I realised that I had made snapshots of my thoughts by writing them down. Checking the manuscript for typos, I found ideas and passions which had gripped me for an afternoon and then evaporated. By re-reading, I was able to pull them back from the ether. And so I began to keep a journal.

Whatever gripped me, I noted down. Frequently some research followed, and occasionally my opinions would veer off on wild tacks as I discovered vast new resources of material on the internet. More and more, my jottings led me back through the galleries of people I had met and known, from my first encounter with celebrity – an audience with Sophia Loren – to Michael Jackson's astonishing concert and party to celebrate 30 years as a solo artist – just hours before tragedy struck New York, in another moment which we will experience endlessly for the rest of our lives.

The material in this book has been sifted from my journal amongst other sources. This explains its episodic nature but has also enabled me to grasp and share feelings and experiences that have been important to me, and to keep the immediacy of my feelings and thoughts. In writing them I have learned much about the people I love. Most of all, I have learned that, without other people, I am nothing. Because of this, my book is dedicated to Hanna and to Shipi, to Natalie and to Daniel, to Mutti and to the spirit of my father, Tibor. With eternal love to all of them.

PART 1

Controversial Encounters

I have always encouraged controversy around my own career.

If scientists found convincing explanations for the physics behind metal-bending and telepathy, my powers would be commonplace. A century ago, when the Wright brothers were pioneering powered flight, a jumbo jet would have looked a ludicrous piece of engineering, the triumph of superstition over science. One day, the same will be true of the mysteries of the human mind.

Some people achieve controversy effortlessly – politicians such as Ariel Sharon, villains like Ronnie Biggs, pop stars such as Eminem. These are my Controversial Encounters.

Being Jewish

I don't very much care if you think I'm a fake. After 30 years of proving my powers and at least 11,000 bent spoons, I am used to sceptics. Many people would prefer to call me a liar than to admit they might have been wrong about the paranormal.

You can think what you like – if you imagine I'm a trickster, I'll happily try to prove you wrong, but I can't help it if you refuse to accept scientific evidence and hard facts.

Your thoughts are one matter – your words are another. Publish an attack on me and my honesty, claim that I am a conjuror or a fraud, and I will force you to retract. If that means a court battle, I will fight. And I do fight, frequently.

Friends sometimes advise me to be less litigious. They say that if I truly don't mind whether one person regards me as a cheat, I shouldn't trouble to prevent that person from speaking out. Freedom of speech, they say, first amendment, sticks and stones.

But they're missing the point. I accept I can't convince all of the people all of the time – but that doesn't mean I'm going to give up in disgust, and refuse to convince anyone. If I allow a few vocal sceptics to broadcast their contempt at will, then the hundreds of millions of people who don't have much of an opinion about Uri Geller either way will soon assume that there's no longer any controversy, that the matter is settled, that I am not psychic, that I have been lying all these years.

The most important opinion about Uri Geller is my own. You don't have to agree with it, but take care if you decide to challenge it.

This is not the stance of an egomaniac. Anyone with any self-respect will make the same stand, 'Think what you like, but watch what you say.'

I felt strong sympathy for the television magnate Michael Grade when the Chief Rabbi declared that Grade was not Jewish, because his mother was a gentile. The law is based on the Halakhah, which ordains that Jewish descent must be traced down the maternal line: 'Your son by an Israelite woman is called your son, but your son by a heathen woman is not called your son' (B.Kid, 68b).

Halakhah or hokum, the Chief Rabbi's remark crosses the line. It goes beyond opinion – it is commanding other people to revise their own most fundamental opinions of a man's personality. It must be challenged because, if Grade ignored the attack, many people would assume he simply has no defence.

He did hit back, and angrily: 'If people want to live their lives the way it was 2,000 years ago, I say good luck to them. It's wonderful. Don't try to impose it on me.'

That sentiment precisely matches mine. For Grade, however, it was just the first salvo. 'Don't try to tell me I'm not a Jew,' he said. 'I'll decide. When the Gestapo knocked on the doors in the middle of the night, did they say, "Oh are you a liberal Jew? You don't have to get on the train. You're not Jewish. You're only half Jewish."'

His sarcasm veils a serious message. Being Jewish – or being psychic – is often a matter of whom you ask. The rabbis might sniff at a Jew's credentials – the Nazis never did. The media have rarely probed too deeply either.

Charlie Chaplin famously refused to deny 'accusations' throughout his career that he was a Jew – first a Jewish draft-dodger in World War One, then a Jewish profiteer in the depression, then a Jewish communist during the McCarthy era. Chaplin's courageous belief, which could have cost him his success, was that his religion was nobody else's business, and that there was no particular shame in being a Jew, any more than being a Christian had any especial merit.

As it happened, his mother was not Jewish and for most of his life Chaplin was an atheist. The rabbis would never have called him a Jew – but Hitler would have paid anything to see the 'Little Tramp' branded with a yellow star and herded onto a wagon bound for Auschwitz.

I should explain I have nothing to gain by speaking out for Grade – quite the opposite. When he was head of Channel 4 he commissioned an *Equinox* documentary which included a vicious assault on my character. In the absence of any substantial evidence against me, the film-makers used relentlessly negative imagery.

The programme made no firm accusations and presented no hard facts, but its insinuations were so powerfully framed that many viewers were left with the definite impression that I had been unmasked, exposed, debunked.

I lodged a formal complaint, and made my point at a tribunal. I wrote to Michael Grade, and he did not answer. The broadcasting bigwig was crossed off the long list of people I would want to sit next to at dinner.

My dispute with him and his programme-makers is in the past. His fight with people who would deny him his right to be a Jew is right here in the present, and it is a fight which has powerful implications for countless people. I have no doubt at all, and I'm happy to declare that of course Michael Grade is a Jew. But likewise, I hope that there are others who respect his beliefs and his lifestyle, in the same way that people I hope do mine.

Eminem

I made the mistake of telling my lawyer I was planning to write a piece about Eminem in my newspaper column. I had met Eminem at the Reading festival earlier in the year and found him to be polite and amiable. Laura didn't have any legal problems about the newspaper article...just a major moral objection.

Laura is twenty years younger than me, divorced, living in Philadelphia with her eight-year-old son, handling a patent issue for me. Her family was not well-off when she and her brothers were growing up in Pittsburgh, she told me, but she worked hard through school, went to college and joined a law firm.

She married one of the associates, also Jewish, a fast-tracker five years her senior. He had a cocaine habit, which became a drug abuse problem, which became a domestic violence problem. Now you know about Laura. She's nice, I like her.

I think she likes me a lot less since I told her I was writing about Eminem, the Detroit rapper who has been nominated for four Grammys. He caused a minor furore with a handful of British concerts earlier this year.

'What, are you calling to get him kicked out of the country?' Laura laughed. 'We don't want him back – you can keep him.'

'I think he's great. Like Bob Dylan with a very foul mouth.'

There was a long pause, the kind of pause you hear from lawyers when they disagree totally with what you just said but they don't want to lose your account.

The single mother won out over the patent lawyer.

'Are you serious? This is a guy who raps about raping his ten-year-old sister and slitting his wife's throat? And you're comparing him to Dylan?'

Over the years, I've learned about arguing with lawyers – when they hit you with a devastating argument, don't make any concessions. If you bend a little, they'll tear the ground away from you and rip you to shreds.

I'd said I thought Eminem was great, and I'd meant it. I couldn't back away from that.

Eminem loves words. They're about the only thing he does have any affection for, except perhaps his four-year-old daughter, Hayley. His blistering articulacy is combined with a gift for mimicry – he acts out all the characters in his verbal vignettes, and every one of them stands out.

It's like a Peter Sellers remake of *Psycho*, with Sellers wielding the knife and wearing Janet Leigh's blonde wig too.

Alfred Hitchcock makes a great defence for Eminem, and I use it on Laura: 'I love a good horror movie, but that's because I know it's not reality. When a girl is slaughtered in the shower, that might be the director's unspeakable fantasy, but it never really happened.

'And when Eminem fantasises about dragging his wife to a remote place and cutting her throat – it didn't happen. She's still alive.'

'What about the women who aren't?' Laura shot back. 'What about the women who did get their throats cut by their boyfriends?'

'Nobody kills because they heard a song, just like nobody becomes a serial murderer because they saw a movie. These things are reflections.'

'But it's not your reflection, is it?' she said. 'I mean, God forbid! You don't see yourself in Eminem, do you?'

Not in the violence, no, I don't. In fact, the violence and the bigotry, the sneering and the libels, quickly overwhelm you and become depressing. Eminem's eight-million-selling album, *The Marshall Mathers LP*, is a hard record to hear from start to finish. And harder still to return to.

The hatred is directed most of all at himself, and then at the women around him – his mother, his child's mother, the groupies. And there's much abuse poured on homosexual men, though Sir Elton John championed him at the Grammys when the two duetted on Eminem's touching, sensitive – yes, and violent, and filthy-mouthed – song, *Stan*.

'What if the bigotry was anti-Jewish?' demanded Laura. 'What if he was chanting about dragging a Jew to a deserted wood and cutting her throat, and acting that out? Would that make a difference to you?'

In fact there are hints of racism in the lyrics. In 'The Way I Am', he describes the St Columbine murders, 'When a Jew's getting bullied and shoots up his school . . .'

One of the schoolboy gunmen in Littleton, Colorado, two years ago was Jewish. So what? His religion had nothing to do with the massacre. Why mention it, unless there is a connection in Eminem's mind – maybe unconscious – between Jews and alienation.

I can imagine him spilling vitriol on religious faith, the way he does on other people's sexual freedom. Would I still compare him to Dylan then?

Yes, I'd have to. There's insight and poetic power in his songs which can't be denied. Or condoned. It just has to be heard. Eminem is almost unique, coming from a poor white background to seize a predominantly black style of music and electrify it with his charisma.

The last guy to do that was Elvis Presley. Also bigoted, also confused. Also brilliant.

It's the Presley model which I believe best predicts Mathers' future career. Elvis grew to hate his fame. He didn't relate to it. No one had told him he was a genius when he was driving a truck. Elvis tried to escape into normality, joining the Army, and then plunging into a doomed relationship with Priscilla.

Eminem repeatedly threatens his listeners with vitriolic abuse or physical assault if they approach him on the street when he's with his daughter. But when he has achieved a break with fame, he'll need to regain that aggravation and adulation if he wants to return to the 'circus' of the music industry. He won't want it, but he'll need it.

And, if he wants his music to be heard, he'll want radio play. And superbowl gigs. And multi-million-dollar one-night-stands in the casinos.

Eminem plays Las Vegas? It's going to happen.

Gay marriages

I was moved and honoured beyond words when two dear friends asked me to marry them. I would be their minister in a service at dusk at the edge of the ocean, a declaration before God to all their family and friends that they loved each other, that they wanted to devote all their days to each other and to raising their own family.

I have known one of them since the late Eighties, an acquaintance forged during some now-forgotten writ or countersuit. Brought up in an Orthodox background, he is an unusually spiritual man for an LA lawyer, with a spiritual creed that is unusual in any profession or country.

I will call him 'Jacob', because the core of his beliefs, as he has carefully explained them to me, is that life is a ladder which we can climb to a higher self – or descend, into a moral morass.

He has lived with his partner, who follows a more conventional Jewish pattern of worship with unfussy

13

earnestness, for four years. I have dined with them a dozen times, and I know they will make wonderful parents. I'll call Jacob's partner 'Elliot'.

They're gay, of course. But it isn't that which makes me doubt whether I should perform their wedding ceremony.

If they simply wanted to be married, that could be done within Judaism. The Central Conference of American Rabbis, whose decisions affect 1.5 million US Jews, agreed earlier this year to support any rabbi who officiated at same-sex weddings.

This bold move was warmly welcomed – the predictable voices of disapproval were widely ignored. 'We're all incredibly proud of the Reform movement for taking the stand,' said Rabbi Jay Perlman of Temple Share Emeth Congregation in Creve Couer. 'The rabbis' statement recognises the dignity and humanity of every single person.'

It's not only in the US. In Canada, Rabbi Michael Levenson is offering gay marriages at his Temple Shalom in Winnipeg. Jacob and Elliot could enjoy a kosher wedding, if that was what they wanted.

I've talked at length to my family and two or three close friends, searching deeply to find the right decision. One friend, a married woman, argued forcefully that I must perform the service, as an act of love to Jacob and Elliot, and as an act of honour to the 100,000 gay men thrown into concentration camps by the Nazis.

There are less than a dozen survivors now who wore the 'pink triangle', a badge of the worst degradation and persecution. One historian, Dr Klaus Muller, has written: 'Marked with a pink triangle, they were the lowest of the low. There was no support network like there was for political or Jewish prisoners. They were put into slave labour squads, subjected to torture and some to terrible medical experimentation.'

Another friend asked me if, subconsciously, I had doubts about the marriage because I knew Jacob and Elliot were intending to adopt children. My answer came instantly and confidently: 'They'll make great parents. No kid could ask for two better dads.'

I know they'll have the support of adoption agencies and courts in California – I am proud that Israel too would offer recognition to them as parents. The story of Matan Berner-Kadish, a four-year-old Jerusalem boy with two mothers, has shown the world Israel's depth of love for the family.

Matan has an American-speaking Mommy called Nicole, and a Hebrew-speaking Ima called Ruth. He is biologically Ruth's child, by artificial insemination from a sperm donor, and he has a baby brother, called Naveh, born to Nicole.

The Israeli High Court has ordered its government to register Nicole as Matan's second mother – a ruling which echoes earlier court cases against El Al, Israel's national airline and the army, awarding benefits to gay partners.

One judge on the three-man panel dissented. Judge Abd al-Rahman Zouabi said he felt the decision sanctioned an 'abnormal family unit'.

If love is abnormal, if caring for two small children is abnormal, if the need to declare lifelong devotion is abnormal – then the idea of normality terrifies me.

We saw a nasty glimpse of old-fashioned normality at the Western Wall recently, after Israel's parliament passed a bill threatening seven years' imprisonment to any woman praying aloud at the site of the Second Temple.

Dozens of women came to defy the law, which directly contradicts a Supreme Court ruling earlier this year. As the women gave praise to God, there were men jeering and yelling 'Shame' and 'Quiet' at them. At least four men had brought eggs to throw at the protestors.

What kind of law must be enforced by hurling eggs at

women in prayer? To any sane person, isn't that abnormal? Love between two people, of whatever gender, and a mutual longing for children – what could be more normal?

With so much good on their side, and so much that is bad set against them, surely Jacob and Elliot deserve the wedding ceremony of their choice? I have read the vows they have prepared, and I know the beauty of the Pacific shoreline setting they have chosen.

And yet I wrote to tell them that I could not act as minister, and phoned to explain my decision. I am a friend who loves them, but there is nothing in my being which qualifies me to intercede for them with God.

A minister must be a man or woman of spiritual authority – or legal authority, such as a registrar or a ship's captain. I am a maverick, not an authority figure. I am a friend, not a guru.

I cannot marry Jacob and Elliot. But nothing will prevent me, if they will permit me as a friend, from standing on that beach to witness their vows.

Who killed Rabin?

There's been a rumour for 35 years that Lee Harvey Oswald did not kill Jack Kennedy. It's so powerful that other news stories have become infected. The deaths of Marilyn Monroe, Robert Maxwell, Princess Diana, Pope John Paul, Jim Morrison and Martin Luther King Jnr are all made mysterious by Kennedy-style conspiracy theories.

Anyone could have predicted that, when Israeli Prime Minister Yitzhak Rabin was murdered on 4 November 1995, by a student radical, the Kennedy conspiracy would infect this killing too. You didn't have to be psychic. There would be hidden gunmen, secret service plots, inexplicable wounds, the inevitable amateur video footage.

What no one could foresee was that the conspiracy might be real. Deadly real. Journalist Barry Chamish, editor of the political intelligence report *Inside Israel*, has put the evidence under a microscope, and found facts that appear to leave no room for question.

17

Rabin was murdered. Police and medical reports obtained by Chamish show the PM was shot point-blank in the chest. The video of ultra-rightist Yigal Amir, flashed round the world by news stations, shows him firing at Rabin from behind.

How can a shot in the back become a fatal chest wound?

'The conspiracy is proved beyond a shadow of doubt,' Chamish told me. 'This isn't a conspiracy theory, it's a crime exposé. My country has sunk into such sick criminality it is unbelievable.'

Chamish in full flow is an impressive sight. He's a bearlike man with restless eyes and a ferocious energy that makes him punch home his argument with swinging, driving gestures. He crashes through objections and doubts like a 38-tonne juggernaut loaded with facts. This can be counter-productive – no one is right all of the time, and there are too many insoluble mysteries in every crevice of Israel's political history to allow anyone to be certain about anything. But without that conviction, that infallibility, Chamish could not spread his message. And it's taking hold – he claims to have convinced more than 30 per cent of Israelis.

The official version has anti-peace protestor Amir, an activist with the Organisation of Jewish Warriors (Eyal), stalking Rabin at a Tel Aviv rally, slipping behind him and gunning him down with two bullets – the second fired as bodyguards wrestled the assassin to the ground. Fatally wounded, Rabin is bundled into his limousine, but dies that night in Ichilov Hospital.

We see it on the video – the figure in the crowd, the gunflash, the confusion, the scramble to get Rabin into his car. But is that what we *really* see?

Chamish, taking the evidence frame by frame, says not. He points to the bodyguards – why did they step out of the way as they approached Amir? They were allegedly warned of an impending attack. Surely they could not have been briefed to slacken at this crucial moment. Could they?

He points to the gunflash – why does it explode several feet from the end of Amir's arm? Why does it appear to be fired with a left-handed action, when Amir is right-handed? Surely this footage was not doctored before release. Was it?

He points to Rabin. At the instant a bullet fatally injures him, severing his spine, the Prime Minister turns quizzically. He looks over his shoulder, as though a noise has distracted him – the noise of blank cartridges, for instance. He walks on. A man with a severed spine walks on. Surely he was not uninjured here – only to be shot dead later. Was he?

Chamish points to the car. The driver and the bodyguard testified there was no one inside. Why then do Foreign Minister Shimon Peres and his bodyguards appear to be discussing the car, with its offside rear door wide open, seconds before Amir shoots? Why does the door mysteriously close itself? Surely the car could not have hidden a hitman, Rabin's real killer. Could it?

The mystery becomes mind-boggling when Chamish reminds us Rabin's car took over eight minutes to reach the hospital, just a few hundred yards away. The driver claimed he got lost. Lost? – while the PM bled to death in the back.

The death certificate signed by Dr Mordecai Gutman, one of Rabin's surgeons, stated he was shot through the chest from the front, shattering his spine. Remarks made by Shimon Peres at a memorial confirmed that.

But Amir shot from behind.

Chamish's terrifying conclusion is that the hitman, who must have had the complicity of Israel's Shabbak, the internal secret service, was under orders – maybe from a foreign power. This was not a lone nut killing. But it was bungled.

Rabin, says Chamish, was shot in the back with blanks, and in the chest in his own car, with his bodyguard beside him and his driver at the wheel. And these shots may not have killed him – Chamish believes the coup de grace was executed in Ichilov Hospital.

Why? Why kill Rabin the peace-maker? Because peace could hurt Israel? Because the peace was flagging, and Rabin had to be replaced? Because Rabin had offended some international power-broker?

Here we are back in the shadowy realm of conspiracy theories. But we ask the questions because we fear the truth – that Chamish's version is the only possible explanation. In my opinion this was a history changing event.

Rehavam Ze'evi

The assassination of Revaham Ze'evi shocked me. I believed in the aura of invincibility which cloaked him. Ze'evi himself believed this aura made him bullet-proof, even if he would not say as much to his comrades – the contempt which he showed for the sensible precaution of keeping his bodyguards beside him at all times spoke louder than any words.

He often carried a miniature sub-machine gun, as much because he liked the gun as for any protection it offered him. But on the day he died he was unarmed, even though he knew there were many people at his hotel who had excellent reason to hate him.

There were, of course, many Palestinian workers on the hotel staff – the same people that Ze'evi proposed should be expelled from the country. He once said: 'We should get rid of the ones who are not Israeli citizens the same way you get rid of lice.'

That remark, as Ariel Sharon suggested at Ze'evi's funeral,

may reveal a deep love of his country – or his vision of how Israel should be – but it speaks of no love for his fellow human beings. It may well be that Ze'evi barely regarded Arabs as human, even though he spoke good Arabic.

Hours before his assassination, he remarked to his wife that he thought he was being watched. Yet he did not pick up his gun, or even the phone. He relied on his invincibility, which he regarded as a gift directly from God.

This same aura was thought by almost all Americans to cloak the USA. Their spymasters, in the weeks before 11 September, heard numerous declarations by Muslim militants that 'something big' was coming. Osama bin Laden announced in a rare interview that an event was planned which would rock the West to its foundations.

They heard, but they did not listen. We all believed in our invincibility. That's what made the atrocity so shocking – that we could be hurt so badly, and so easily.

I met Ze'evi more than 30 years ago; in fact, he helped to make my career. At the end of the Sixties, when I was earning a living as a male model – yes, it's true that I modelled underpants, and I happen to think I looked pretty good in them – I was also making a name for myself as a paranormalist on the home party circuit.

Home parties were one of the things I missed most when I left Israel. The English taste for dinner parties and the American enthusiasm for barbecues are pale imitations of the Jewish get-together. Perhaps only a people who cares so passionately about families can take a social gathering this seriously.

My first party was thrown by a photographer who was handling one of my fashion shoots. I bent a spoon for him, and he asked if I'd come over and do the same for his guests. 'Sure,' I said, 'if you'll pay me.' It didn't occur to me that I was launching a career.

That party led to more, and word-of-mouth spread, so I was quickly drafted up through the social strata. Within a few weeks I was bending spoons not for models and journalists but for politicians and commentators – I didn't see much of a difference then, and I see less of one now.

When Rehavam Ze'evi called me, I told him my fee was around £15, a small fortune to me at the time. I went to his home, which was furnished exclusively with Israeli artefacts – Roman coins from the time of Herod, perfume jars and wine dishes from Biblical times, photographs and paintings of the Holy Land. I called him Gandhi, as everyone did – an affectionate reference to his shaven head, and an ironic nod to his politics.

I asked everyone to sit around me in a circle. The fact that Golda Meir and Moshe Dayan were there didn't faze me: I believed then that I, like these national leaders, was a person of international importance. Or at least I would be, when things got going.

My routine was to explain something of the powers of the mind, and then to ask for a telepathy volunteer. Golda Meir selected herself, and I sent her to the toilet to make her drawing.

I received it instantly – she was a natural transmitter – and reproduced her Star of David to the millimetre. Then I bent a spoon for Ze'evi, while he held it in his own hands. He seemed to regard it as a natural phenomena, and I sensed at once that this man was aware of his own formidable powers of intuition.

Most soldiers are – though the most open-minded group of people are, I believe, pilots. Perhaps the fact that daily they use subtle laws of physics to defy a grosser law, aerodynamics over gravity, enables them to see the reason-defying powers of the human psyche.

Golda Meir wanted to know if I could see the future. She

asked how many more wars the country faced, and I predicted we would sign a peace treaty with Egypt before we made peace with other Arab nations.

Other questions and answers followed. 'Could I use my mind to influence the stock market?' asked a broker. 'Could I tell whether a witness was lying in the dock?' asked a judge. 'Could I find buried antiquities by dowsing over a map?' asked Dayan.

Ze'evi did not want my predictions. There was only one accurate outlook on life, he knew, and that was his own.

Dayan, however, did put me to work, towards the end of his service as Defence Minister. I located archaeological treasures for him, which he then dug up and displayed in his home, which was almost a museum.

It was a practical, enjoyable and harmless pastime. Looking back, I suspect that it was also illegal. Gandhi would not have approved.

My mother's abortions

I was one of nine children. My eight older brothers and sisters were all aborted before I was born. My father did not want them, so they died. A father can have that sort of power.

Why he let me come into the world alive, I don't know. He relented once. For my mother, that was enough. She wasn't asking any questions. My father has been dead for over 20 years, so I can't ask him any questions either, though I learned of this private holocaust only recently.

Holocaust is not too violent a word. Eight children, killed before they even possessed names, constitute a tribal slaughter, a systematic attempt to rip out one chapter from the book of mankind.

If I had not been allowed to live, or my mother had never spoken of her tragedy, the slaughter would have been complete. My brothers and sisters would have been utterly unremembered – they could simply not have existed. This is the way holocausts are supposed to work.

In his memoir of Auschwitz, *The Truce*, Primo Levi remembers a crippled boy of three called Hurbinek. The child could not speak, and one of the women had given him the meaningless name out of pity.

Though he was fiercely alive, he was unable to communicate anything – what his real name was, who his parents had been, what he needed. He died in this state, dumb, and Levi noted, 'Nothing remains of him – he bears witness through these words of mine.'

Levi knew his responsibility to the ones who did not survive. They were to bear witness to the holocaust through him.

I wish I could claim my brothers and sisters are alive through me, that my soul comprises their souls and that their flames flicker in my flame. But the simple fact is that nothing remains of them, except my words and my mother's thoughts.

They could not speak, and they cannot bear witness, except through me.

There is a man who, although he is untrained, believes himself to be a rabbi, named Uzi Meshulam. He is imprisoned near Netanyah for trying to bear witness for 400 Yemeni children, forcibly parted from their families in the Forties and Fifties, to be sold.

Operation Magic Carpet, the evacuation of 50,000 Jews from Yemen to the newborn state of Israel, yielded an unexpected benefit for someone. Was it the government, the refugee camp officials, the doctors or the army who arranged for children to disappear from nursery wards and reappear in the European and American homes of childless Jewish couples?

Whoever was responsible, he acted like a father who orders his wife to have abortions. His power was absolute.

The fact of this trade in human beings, which was so nearly forgotten forever, cannot now be ignored. Rabbi

Meshulam, through his often desperate attempts to bear witness, has seen to that.

The Yemeni parents were told their children had died and been buried before their families could see the corpses.

The evacuation had been conducted amid chaos, and fatalities were inevitable. Many of the refugee children were malnourished. Yet it seems strange that, according to Rabbi Meshulam and the Yemen Jewish group Mishkan Oahlim, it was the fair-skinned children who died.

Fair-skinned children were more easily absorbed into the families of the Ashkenazi communities, who originated in Eastern Europe.

When mass graves at the Sha'ar Menashe and Karkur Ein-Irron cemeteries in Israel were opened not long ago, they were empty. So where are the children now?

They will be about my age, wholly unaware of their true parentage, as I was ignorant of my siblings' existence. If Rabbi Meshulam, who has suffered appalling conditions in jail, is denied the right to freedom, then the truth will never come out.

No one will know who stole these children, or who sold them, and to whom. They will carry their secret tragedy with them all their lives, and not ever be aware of its existence.

Semitic genes

A dear friend, one of the few people who was kind to me during an awful childhood year as a kibbutz boy, called me recently. Her name is Sarah, and she is a fervent woman. I told her once that, if she had been born Russian she would have been a Cossack, and if she had been born Japanese she would have been a Samurai.

But she was born Jewish, on a kibbutz, and she is an Arab-hater.

Sarah was the girl who chased off the bigger boys when they threw sticks at me, and saved handfuls of bread from her plate when I was too sullen and sulky to eat with the families. She spoke to me like I was a little stupid, a city boy who would never understand how human nature was when it had been stripped down to raw components. She still speaks to me that way.

In Sarah's eyes, it is an Israeli's duty to detest the war-loving people of Syria and Iraq, the spies of Jordan and

Lebanon, the Saudi and Kuwaiti gluttons. To hate especially the cheating Palestinians, the lying land-robbers who hide behind a shield of children.

She tells me that to spare them an inch of trust or sympathy would be a betrayal of her ideals, and her parents' hard work, and the dreams of her whole race. She asks me, mildly, reasonably, whether the ordinary people of Europe, including the British, spared an inch of sympathy for the Jews who were obliterated by the Nazis.

Today I told her about the findings of Michael Hammer at the University of Arizona in Tucson, which showed the Semitic gene pool has been almost constant for the past 4,000 years. Since the time of the Pharoahs, the children of Abraham have maintained their racial characteristics.

The essential factors in our biological make-up are no different today than they were in early Biblical days. Long before Solomon and David, our nature was defined.

Sarah, naturally, was delighted by the report. She questioned me closely as I explained that Hammer had studied and compared the genes of more than 1,300 men and boys from all over the Semitic world. The seven Jewish groups – the Ashkenazi, the Roman, the North African and the Ethiopian, the Kurdish, Iraqi, Iranian and Yemenite – all showed a consonance of the Y chromosome so clearly that only one conclusion could be drawn: they all shared a common male ancestor.

There was a patriarch. And the Bible calls him Abraham.

Excited and amused, Sarah still tried to keep her control of our conversation and the whole friendship. She is always in charge when we talk. 'Anyone could have told you this,' she said. 'Read your Torah, we don't need genetics to prove the scriptures.'

'I have read the Torah,' I said. 'And I think Abraham

had two sons. Right? It wasn't only Isaac. That's where the Jewish line started.

'But Isaac had an older brother. Ishmael, am I right? And the Arabs claim common descent from Ishmael, so Arab and Jew, we're all descended from Abraham. Tell me if I've got this wrong, but doesn't a devout Muslim revere Abraham, El Khalil, the Friend of God, above anyone in the Bible?'

'You ask me about the Koran, I have no idea,' Sarah snapped, 'but I can tell you that anything an Arab says to a Jew is a lie.'

'It isn't what Arabs say. I'm still with the University of Arizona. The geneticists looked at 29 populations. Not just Jews – Palestinians, Syrians, Lebanese, the Druze, Saudis and Semitic clusters in Gambia and Germany and Russia and Eygpt and Austria...even here in Britain. And along the Y chromosome line, we are all virtually identical.

'Listen to this,' I said, 'this is Dr Harry Ostrer, who is director of the Human Genetics Program at New York University School of Medicine: "Jews and Arabs are all really children of Abraham." That's the scientific view.'

Sarah was silent for a long time. 'Like you said,' she answered at length, 'it's all in the Torah.' Another pause. 'But how come we don't diverge more over 4,000 years?'

The single father of all these nations, so clearly described in Holy literature for thousands of years, seems an impossibility to a twenty-first century mind – even one steeped in orthodoxy and insular politics. But the Tucson study is not the only piece of research to show that Earth's six billion people are all descended from a very small family.

Biologist Brian Sykes, Professor of Human Genetics at Oxford's Institute of Molecular Medicine, believes all Westerners are descended from just seven women who lived between 8,000 and 45,000 years ago – well before the time of

Abraham. He is so confident that maternal or mitochondrial DNA from one of these seven can be found in any European that he has given each of the types a name – Ursula, Xenia, Tara, Helena, Katrine, Valda and Jasmine.

The last, Jasmine, is the most likely mother of most Semites – born in Syria after the Ice Age, Jasmine's people learned that seeds grew into plants and so became the planet's first farmers. Animals were domesticated, instead of being hunted in the wild. And nomadic traditions passed away.

Jasmine's tribe settled in the Middle East. After thousands of years a man was born who rejected pagan gods and worshipped the one true deity – even willing to sacrifice his beloved son. And the rest, as they say, is scripture.

Domestic violence

So you don't like Eminem. That's OK: I am disturbed by my own admiration for him. But most of all, every woman who has argued with me about it – and with only two exceptions, most of the complaints I've encountered come from women – was angry at the abuse, physical, emotional and verbal, which had been meted out in her own past.

Domestic violence happens everywhere, in families of every race and religion. I saw my father abuse my mother and when I was a child it seemed brutally unique – now I know it is an endless epidemic, all the more vicious for being hidden.

At least one in every ten readers of a national paper will suffer a physical attack from a close relative that week, or an emotional assault so cruel that it will seem worse than a beating. That's this week, and every week. That's at least one in ten – and probably twice as many.

Ronit Abraham, who works at the Centre of Violence Against Women in Tel Aviv, where 80 volunteers offer support and counselling in Hebrew, Arabic and Russian, says last year's figures show domestic violence afflicts 20 per cent of Israeli families.

'This we can conclude from the amount of incoming calls to our national hotline telephone number, but of course there are many victims who do not call us,' Abraham says.

The international statistics are equally sickening. The FBI estimates that four women are killed by their partners in America every day. More than 20,000 assaults are reported every week, and far more go unseen and unheard. One Philadelphia study found that a fifth of women treated in emergency wards were victims of domestic violence.

In the US a woman is beaten every 15 seconds, with 50,000 women seeking restraining orders annually and 50 per cent of homeless women and children the victims of domestic assaults.

It is not only the fist in the face, the push that sends you reeling and falling. It is the sudden kick, the sharp slap, plates and cutlery hurled, the hot iron held an inch from skin. Choking, tripping, pinching, squeezing, a shove at the top of the stairs, a lurch on the car accelerator when the passenger door is wide open.

In every instance of physical abuse that was ever described to me, there was an element of disguise, a twist that could make the victim say, 'At least he didn't go as far as... that.'

In other words, a deeper, more frightening level of violence is always implicit.

It happens in Japan, where up to 60 per cent of women have been physically assaulted by their partner on at least one occasion. In Ecuador the figures are as bad. In Korea, 38 per cent of women have been battered in the past year. In Beijing, China, 23 per cent of men admit to beating their wives.

Hillary Rodham Clinton told 400 experts from 37

countries at a conference in Washington, 'Domestic violence undermines democracy itself.'

A World Bank study ratified her claim, showing that assaults in the home hurt the global economy as badly as HIV, heart disease or cancer. US businesses lose about $5 billion annually from abuse-related absenteeism, and another $100 million in medical costs.

All these figures prove simply that a woman abused is not alone – even a Jewish woman, who may feel it her duty to preserve the illusion of *shalom bayit*, or peace in the home. Only 10 per cent of Jewish women beaten by their husbands will speak to the rabbi, and on average they will endure the violence five to seven years longer than other wives.

Elaine Weiss, a Clinical Associate Professor at the University of Utah and the author of *Surviving Domestic Violence*, explains, 'I didn't leave, because abuse wasn't supposed to happen to people like me. It happened only to impoverished, uneducated women married to men with names like Billy Bob, who turned into mean drunks on Saturday nights. It certainly didn't happen to nice Jewish girls from upper-middle-class families.'

This quote is taken from www.jewishwomen.org which is also the source for many of my statistics. It's the website of Jewish Women International, an offshoot of B'Nai B'rith which began to fight domestic violence when one of its own members was murdered by her husband in 1988.

The telltale signs of violence in the home may not be bruises. The ugliness shows itself in the victim's low self-esteem, constant apologies at work and willingness to take on endless tasks from friends and neighbours. It adds up to an apparently deliberate martyrdom, but is usually the outer display of a subconscious desire to be low enough to merit the abuse and the beatings.

If you suspect that a friend, colleague or relation is the

victim of violence, do not attempt to be judge and jury. Don't offer advice like, 'Leave him now!' or 'Fight back!' because it isn't you who has to run those risks.

Let your friend talk. Ask questions which get to the core of the problem without colouring the answer. And if you are the victim of violence in the home, focus on this – you are not the only one. There are millions like you. And they will help you.

If Jerry Springer was God

Camera: Wide pan across jeering, baying audience of rough, coarse-faced men and women. They all have wings. And halos.

Music: Big, blaring and beaty.

Titles: Massive, ornate gold lettering thumps into the screen – The Yahweh Springer Show!! And then, spinning for maximum impact, the theme of today's programme – Judgment Day!!!

Camera: Yahweh Springer bounds down the stairs towards the stage, cleaving through the adoring angels like a prophet parting seas. He's average height, with a clipped white beard and shining white locks, but his tanned face looks early 50s, and his hyped-up energy is pure 20-something.

Angels: Yah-weh! Yah-weh! Yah-weh!

Camera: Yahweh Springer, the highest-paid chat show host in the universe, is grasping hands and trading friendly punches with frantic delight as the audience pants to glimpse him. His double-breasted suit glows. Even his multi-coloured tie has its own divine aura.

Yahweh: Thank-you, and if you thought last week's show, 'Hi Honey I'm The Messiah', was going to be hard to top – get this! In tonight's studio we're dishing out eternal damnation! Heavenly retribution! And the ultimate lie detector test! It's... Judgment Day!

Angels: Yah-weh! Yah-weh! Yah-weh!

Yahweh (to fat, confidant-looking businessman in tubular chair onstage): Your name's Company Chairman Eli Goldstein, right?

Businessman: I got nothing to fear.

Yahweh (incredulously): You don't fear me? And you a God-fearing man? Bad start, businessman.

Businessman (suddenly sweating): I did everything just like you said. I kept my family indoors on the Shabbat. I never made out with my wife when she was menstruating.

Angels: Wooo! Wooo-wooo-wooo-wooo!

(Three-second bleep out, as someone in row three, very much in the Prophet Elijah's vicinity, hurls an obscene comment.)

Businessman: Everything I ate was kosher, I never touched unclean – not even a packet of pork scratchings.

Yahweh: Looks like you didn't starve on it.

Businessman: It's my hormones, is it my fault if I got a slow metabolism?

Yahweh: No. But what I want to ask you, is this your fault?

Camera: Backstage, a girl with black hair and dark rings round her eyes is pushed forward by stagehands. Her legs, thin as wire, will barely hold her. She slumps in a chair half-turned to the rabbi's and stares in terror at the howling angels. She is 13 years old.

Businessman: I've never seen this child. Nothing to do

with... (he starts to grin, and lets off a fat, smarmy chuckle) Are you going to suggest this is my illegitimate daughter? The big surprise? Because I got news for you – your researchers have goofed. My private life has been blameless!

Angels: Lie test! Lie test! Lie test!

Businessman: Sure.

(He sits back while a pillar of salt is levelled at his head. The pillar crumbles. Angels cheer and chant, and the businessman grins and brandishes his fists aloft.)

Yahweh: This girl's no relation of yours. She just happens to live ten miles down the road from your Jerusalem apartment...

Businessman: She's Palestinian! Anyone can see that! So maybe I've seen her running around in those roadside gangs – maybe she's hurled a rock at my car once in a while, yeah? What am I supposed to do – get out and pat her on the head?

Yahweh: I don't know if you've seen her before. Well, OK, I do know, because I'm omniscient...

Angels: Yah-weh! Yah-weh! Yah-weh!

Yahweh: ...but what I don't know is this. How come you're well-fed and she's not?

Businessman (baffled): It's the political situation.

Yahweh: OK, I'm not expressing myself very clearly. How come you're well-fed and she's not, and you don't seem to care? This girl sits down, you quite rightly think immediately, 'She's young enough to be my daughter.' And then you decide, 'No, she can't be, and what the hell, she's not Jewish. She's an Arab.' Isn't that what went through your mind?

Businessman: Well...

Yahweh: Am I right?

(He points his microphone at another pillar of salt.)

Businessman: Yes! Yes!

Yahweh: So it doesn't matter if she starves? Just so long as your taxes make certain there's enough government-issue batons and guns, so she doesn't hurl too many rocks at your car? It doesn't matter if none of your taxes goes into her stomach. Right? In fact, you don't want to pay to put one ladle of soup in her bowl. Right?

Businessman (screaming): Haven't I got enough tax to pay for the Jewish state? You want me to care about Muslims too?

(Long series of bleeps as the Prophet Elijah blows his cool and plunges out of of the third row onto the stage, fists flailing. He slaps the businessman's glasses off his face and plants a foot in the large, absorbent stomach before four crew men drag him off and back into the heavenly congregation. Yahweh watches, mouth set in prim disapproval and arms folded.)

Cut to – Yahweh's Final Thought: Judgment's never easy. It's something no deity takes lightly. And believe me – when it comes to your turn, I'll be reading my research carefully. But ask yourself this question now: Am I living by the rules? Or just by the rulebook? Until next week, when we're going to be confronting Noah with his alcohol problem . . . shalom.

End title: Five raucous angels bawl out 'Tell Yahweh he's groovy' to the tune of 'Tell Laura I Love Her'.

Was Hercule Poirot a woman?

'A little man with a face like a rat.' Meet the villain of an Agatha Christie tale. 'In an Empire where rats ruled, he was the king of the rats.'

And guess what religion he was. 'His face gleamed white and sharp in the moonlight. There was the least hint of a curve in the thin nose. His father had been a Polish Jew, a journeyman tailor...'

The year was 1928 – though my paperback edition of *The Mystery of the Blue Train* is 1975, shortly before Dame Agatha's death. Boris Ivanovitch Krassnine, king of rats, was an anarchist, of course. Jew, anarchist, rat – what was the difference in 1928?

Over ten million miles of travelling or more, I have read dozens of Christies. The Poirots are my favourites – I love a character who is not afraid to boast. Miss Marple is self-deprecating, and I have always regarded modesty as an over-rated virtue.

In all those mysteries, I cannot remember that a Jew was ever unmasked as the murderer on the final page. As a villain, clearly stated from the start, Jews appear constantly, at least in the earlier books. They are fixers, fences, plotters, renegades and, obviously, anarchists.

But the murderer must be unsuspected, and Christie probably assumed that all Jews were automatically suspects. Even the better sorts, like Jim Lazarus in *Peril at End House*, 'He's a Jew, of course, but a frightfully decent one.'

Her racism towards blacks was more blatant still. One of her most ingenious plots – one of my favourite detective stories ever – was called *Ten Little Niggers* until an American publisher, in a horribly bigoted stroke of political correctness, changed it to *Ten Little Indians*.

The book now sells as *And Then There Were None*, but the scene of the crimes is still Nigger Island... 'Smelly sort of rock covered with gulls. It had got its name from its resemblance to a man's head – a man with negroid lips.'

This sort of prejudice is impossible to ignore. It stops the reader dead on the page, in a novel that rattles along at 100 pages an hour. But it does not stop the sales. When she died, it was estimated 250 million Christies had been printed, a record beaten only by the Bible and Shakespeare.

Dame Agatha did not set out to preach contempt for Jews and blacks. The attitude was ingrained, subconscious, and it seeped into her writing. Studying four or five of her best novels, I discovered something else about Agatha Christie's subconscious – it moulded her hero in her own likeness, far more than she ever guessed.

When she created Hercule Poirot, the retired Belgian detective with the invincible brain, millions were dying in Belgium. In 1916, six years before publication, Christie was writing:

'Poirot was an extraordinary-looking little man. He was hardly more than five feet four inches, but carried himself with great dignity. His head was exactly the shape of an egg, and he always perched it a little on one side. The moustache was very stiff and military. The neatness of his attire was almost incredible; I believe a speck of dust would have caused him more pain than a bullet wound.'

The 'I' was Captain Hastings, Poirot's dim-but-brave disciple. The detective adored him. Later in this first adventure, *The Mysterious Affair at Styles*, he displays his affection – 'suddenly clasping me in his arms, he kissed me warmly on both cheeks'.

Poirot loved Hastings, but Christie despised Poirot. 'Why,' she asked in the *Daily Mail* in 1938, 'why, why did I ever invent this detestable, bombastic, tiresome little creature?... eternally straightening things, eternally boasting, eternally twirling his moustache and tilting his egg-shaped head... anyway, what is an egg-shaped head?... I am beholden to him financially... On the other hand, he owes his very existence to me.'

Poirot had no lady friends, though he liked to flirt and once, at the end of a cycle of short stories called *The Labours of Hercules*, he sent a bunch of red roses to the villainous Countess Rossakoff.

But he understood women. He knew which men they would desire – usually the bad ones – and what would flatter them most. He knew when they would be loyal, and when treacherous. He even knew, in *Peril at End House*, how best to style their hair, 'To me the natural thing seems to have a coiffure high and rigid – so – and the hat attached with many hatpins – là, là, là-et là!'

And then he gave himself away, 'When the wind blew, it was agony – it gave you the migraine.'

It is not unknown for a woman to live as a man. Two fearsome pirates, Ann Bonny and Mary Read, were revealed as women at their trial, when both claimed to be pregnant.

They were sentenced to death. The secret of soldier Christian Davies's sex was discovered by army surgeons after she was wounded in the battle of Ramilles.

And just 11 years ago jazz pianist and band leader Billy Tipton, the father of three children by adoption, was discovered during his autopsy to have been a woman. He had married three times.

The truth then is shocking and hard to comprehend, but as in all the best Christie it remains the only possible solution. Hercule Poirot was a woman.

Fischer and Hoddle

Bobby Fischer, the greatest chess player in history, the man who won the Cold War with the power of his mind, is now a sad, ranting anti-Semite. For his first interview for more than two years, the self-exiled American went live on a tiny Budapest radio station and undammed a barely coherent torrent of nonsense. 'Those damned Jews are persecuting me,' he repeated again and again.

Presenter Daniel Molner tried to challenge him, asking: 'Aren't you Jewish yourself?' Chicago-born Fischer, whose mother Regina was a Jew, heatedly insisted he was not. He threatened to 'prove it in the toilets'. The station, Radio Calypso, pulled the plug.

It is horrible to realise that Fischer, who abandoned competitive chess in the mid-Seventies rather than defend his world crown, is still tortured by race hatred and paranoia. Something like this should have been expected. Fischer has been spouting master-race claptrap since he was 16. In 1961 he told Ralph Ginzburg: 'There are too many Jews in chess. They seem to have taken away the class of the game. They don't seem to dress so nicely, you know.'

At Sveti Stefan in September 1992, at the height of the Yugoslav civil war, Fischer broke UN sanctions to play a $5,000,000 match against Boris Spassky, the Russian he had beaten 20 years earlier to become world champion. The American told a press conference, 'Soviet communism is basically a mask for Bolshevism, which is a mask for Judaism... "anti-Semitism" is a nonsense term, because my understanding is that the Arabs are also Semites, not only the Jews. I'm definitely not anti-Arab.'

At that conference, Fischer took a letter from the Treasury Department in Washington, warning him not to defy the sanctions against Serbia, and spat on it. He has not been able to return to the US since, and lives in Hungary.

Radio Calypso had to ditch the interview, of course, though it is hard to imagine anyone could be really offended by Fischer's ravings. He was not always like this – I met him at Palo Alto, California, 25 years ago, and was struck by the intense focus of his mind.

His elder sister Joan was married to a scientist, Russell Targ, who was testing me at Stanford Research Institute. Fischer dropped by and I bent a spoon for him. I don't think he was especially impressed – maybe he thought it was a conjuring trick, but when I reproduced an image he had secretly drawn, that startled him. I remember he chose a knight's head, and his telepathic transmission was clear as a radio wave. He wanted to know how he could train his psychic energies to increase his concentration at the board – no one knew in 1973 that Fischer's mental instability would turn him away from the game which was his obsession.

If Fischer had remained world champion and an

American idol, his twisted garbage would disturb me. As it is, I simply hope he can find some peace with himself.

But in another interview, a second international sports figure was also spouting some twisted garbage. I was equally disturbed by another star interview, given by the then English football coach Glen Hoddle, and his remarks about disabled people. Hoddle is another celebrity who wanted to meet me – he and his spiritualist mentor Eileen Drewery visited my home several years ago. In the run-up to the World Cup, I mentioned this in a *News of the World* interview. Hoddle denied it, accused me of lying and said he would sue me.

I didn't receive any writ, and the threat came to nothing. Since my itemised phone bills show clearly how frequently Eileen and I spoke on the phone before their visit, I wasn't exactly concerned about defending my reputation. But I didn't like my children seeing tabloid headlines accusing me of lying.

How would I feel if I had a disability, and my kids read Hoddle's interview in *The Times*? 'You have to come back to learn and face some of the things you have done, good and bad,' he told reporter Matt Dickinson. 'You and I have been physically given two hands and two legs and half-decent brains. Some people have not been born like that for a reason. The karma is working from another lifetime. I have nothing to hide about that. It is not only people with disabilities. What you sow, you have to reap.'

For logic, humanity and emotional depth, that's on a par with Fischer's 'the Jews are persecuting me'. The difference is that any Jew can enjoy chess without having to associate himself with Fischer. But around ten per cent of the English population has some sort of disability. That means perhaps a quarter of England's families are somehow affected, including of course the families of England footballers, former England players, and the countless England fans. Hoddle, inadvertently, and without realising it, was directly insulting all of them.

I believe in karma too, though I understand it as a natural, spiritual force. If you help people and speak kindly, you deserve good things from the world – you might not get them, but at least you will be at peace with yourself. Good karma.

If you let racial hatred grip you, and you despise your country and you fear other nationalities, you will become bitter and lonely and insignificant. Sad karma.

But if you spit on the people you are serving and strut and bluster and sneer, you will destroy your career and lose the respect of your friends. That's the real meaning of bad karma.

Ronnie Biggs

Ronnie Biggs would have been free a long time ago. That's what tortured him. Of the twelve Great Train Robbers jailed in 1964, ten were let out in the mid-Seventies. Two escaped: Charlie Wilson was recaptured and served his time. Only Biggs remained on the run, forced to live out a lifelong punishment in the the name of freedom.

I met him in 1994, when he was still a strong, vital man – though his hair was white and his puffy face was ravaged by alcohol. My son, who was in his early teens, and I had flown from Chile, where I had been shooting a TV show, to Rio.

I wanted Daniel to see the train station, where thousands of street children beg for centavos. I wanted him to see the favelas, the slums, where even the children with houses to shelter them must fight for every scrap of food. I wanted him to know that poverty beyond imagination was the norm, not the exception, so that he would not take his own Western wealth for granted.

Most of all, I wanted to nurture the powerful sense of justice which was already visible in his soul like a streak of iron. And this I did, for the poverty of Brazil is a crime against mankind.

And then we went to meet a very different kind of criminal.

On the plane from Santiago we met a woman, one of the cabin crew, who was deeply interested in the powers of the mind. We got to talking about Rio's most famous Englishman, and she told us that Biggs was also interested in telepathy and psychic energy.

She didn't know him but she knew people who did, and she thought she could arrange a meeting. That was more difficult than it sounded, because although Biggs made his living by entertaining strangers and charging them to pose for photos with him, he was also a wary man.

He had been the subject of more than one kidnap attempt by bounty hunters and one bid had succeeded in getting him as far as Mexico, where extradition proceedings broke down. Though a Jewish psychic with an adolescent son seemed an unlikely kidnapper, he may have been afraid that I was working for the Government, under orders to hypnotise him and bring him home.

His friends brought us by a deliberately tortuous route to his spectacular house overlooking the city. High on a hillside, it was a miniature palace, verdant, and opulent with marble. Biggs greeted us like a gangland king, which he never was, and invited us to a light lunch with heavy refreshments.

His foot was bandaged, and it was this factor which had convinced him to meet me – he was hoping I could perform a small miracle of healing on a broken bone which refused to set. I told him that he was the healer, not I, and that all I could do was act as the catalyst, to trigger his own healing energies.

Biggs was an intelligent man behind the bad man's bluster, and he intuitively understood what I was saying. He assumed a relaxed pose and closed his eyes, focusing his imagination on fantasies of a mended bone in a healthy foot.

After a while he said, without opening his eyes: 'I ain't thinking of my foot no more. Know what I'm thinking of? A pint of best.'

'So imagine that you are walking into an English pub,' I said, 'without your stick, your foot free from pain. And you go up to the bar and put that foot on the rail and order that pint of best, and when you drink it down in one swallow the dark brown liquid turns gold and flows through your bones into your foot. And there is great strength in your foot, and the love you have for that beer fills your foot and energises it.'

He laughed, and then his eyes flickered open. He looked at me with suspicion and not a little malevolence. 'What you trying to do?'

'What matters,' I answered calmly, 'is what you're trying to do. To heal yourself.'

He shook his head like an old lion. 'Nah, what I'm trying to do is keep out of England. And I don't want you hypnotising me to come home with you.'

'I'm not trying to hypnotise you, and anyway, I couldn't do it against your will. But why do you have to try so hard to stay here?'

'Because I want to go back. I want it bad. I miss it so much, you couldn't understand. This ain't the lap of luxury here. It ain't even exile. It's a prison. A cell.'

'A bigger cell than the one that's waiting for you in England,' I reminded him. 'And there's no blue sky and yellow beach there. No pools and girls and wine.'

'Thanks,' he said sarcastically, 'I'd forgotten that. So you'd stay here then?'

I looked round. It was beautiful. But he was right – it was a prison. 'No,' I told him, 'I'd catch the next flight home.'

'That's what I should do. But I can't. I'm scared, and I'm homesick, and I'm in pain. I don't have good health no more. I'm scared of dying here. But it'll have to get much worse before I get the nerve to escape this time. See, what I'm doing here is serving my sentence. It ain't like a sentence the judge gives you.'

'Is it God's sentence?' I asked him.

He looked at me. 'Didn't expect a Jew to understand,' he remarked casually.

'Jews know nothing about exile, of course,' I said, repaying his sarcasm.

'Right,' he nodded slowly. 'But you Jews found your Promised Land, didn't yer?'

'After a long journey.'

He looked out across the city. 'I can feel this foot healing. When it's strong enough to stand on, maybe I'll start my own journey. Back to my own Promised Land.'

Now his exile, like his days of villainy, is over. I hope he finds peace, if not here, then on the other side.

Ariel Sharon

Clearly there was something going on. Security were crawling all over our apartment building and it wasn't because Rabbi Shmuley Boteach was threatening to throw another of his ground-shaking tantrums.

We walked off the New York sidewalk through the cordon; our host was well-known to the concierge. I'll call him Uli, because that's the name I know him by – when he publishes his blockbusting thrillers, he uses a nom de plume, James Douglas.

Uli asked one of the white-shirted men with the Uzis at their waists: 'What's going on? You got Sharon and Arafat upstairs?'

'Just Sharon,' said the bodyguard.

He wasn't kidding. We knew that Israel's Prime Minister Ariel Sharon was in the States for a high-profile session of hand-shaking with America's new president, George W. Bush but the excursion to Manhattan hadn't been advertised.

I asked Uli whether part of the building was reserved by the CIA for heads of state, but it seemed more likely that Sharon was the guest of a millionaire on the top floor who imported Swiss watches.

Thirty years earlier I met Sharon in extraordinary Cold War circumstances. Now that the hopes of Middle Eastern peace hung by a thread from his hands, I had a chance no less extraordinary to meet him again.

'Call up to his suite and tell him we'd like to drop by,' I said. Uli raised his eyebrows. 'So tell him we'd like to bring Michael Jackson,' I said.

Within 90 minutes we stepped through a corridor of bodyguards and I laid eyes on a man I last saw in 1971 at an Israeli airforce base, when all of us feared that not only Israel but the whole planet could cease to exist at the touch of a button.

I'd been doing a show for fighter pilots at an airfield near the Suez Canal where the front line would have been if the war with Egypt had been overt and not covert. I didn't know that one of our most senior commanders was watching, and it wouldn't have fazed me too much – I was more awed by the focus and fearlessness of the men who were clustered round the stage, the pilots who had proved themselves to be the quickest and most resilient characters in an army which was famed for the dedication of its servicemen.

Sharon shook my hand, asked if the spoonbending was a trick and grunted when I protested that it was a psychic feat which depended on the mind's belief in its own power.

I had a strong sense that this man was himself psychic – that he recognised intuitive impulses in his own make-up and that he was unafraid to act upon them. Very often it is this courage, the readiness to be guided by instinct, that separates the great leaders from the others.

I instantly felt this was a man who could rise to lead Israel. But little did I know that this was also the man who could have led to the start of the intifada by visiting Temple Mount three decades later. In the past few months, following my sudden acceleration to fame, I'd met many impressive people who electrified the dangerous political atmosphere, and it was obvious that Ariel Sharon could be the match of any of them.

I said nothing of the sort, of course. He didn't look like the kind of soldier who would stoop to acknowledge flattery. Instead, I said on an impulse: 'There will be a raid tonight.'

'Where?' asked Sharon, unflustered, like a squadron leader receiving a report from his radar operator.

'Here. Some time before dawn.' I pointed to the precise section of the Suez Canal on a map spread on the wall.

He simply nodded. I was driven away from the airbase, back to Tel Aviv. Later I learned Sharon had ordered a reinforcement to that location and a raid was successfully defeated, without any loss of life, not even an injury.

Thirty years later I was walking into a room to see the same man, seated and eating, older and white-haired but exuding the same calm, magnetic presence. He glanced up and met my eyes for a moment before looking behind me to my companion.

The next quarter of an hour was exhausting. Simply to watch Michael Jackson posing for photographs and signing autographs is a chastening experience. I have thought myself at the centre of whirlwinds when media attention has borne down on me, but all that is nothing compared to the hurricane which Michael carries with him. He is the calm eye of an insane, perfect storm which sweeps up anyone who steps within its howling limits.

I judged in 1971 that Sharon's aura of power was a match for any man's. Here in a city apartment I saw the proof: the only man whose dignity was unscorched by Michael's radiance was Sharon's. They sat together for pictures, and the Prime Minister's aristocratic splendour was the equal of the King of Pop's ephemeral beauty.

Sharon reminded me of another man. He seemed archetypal, and ancient, and infinitely resonant to my memory, but I could not think of whom he reminded me – until Shmuley whispered, 'He looks like every boy's perfect father.'

That was the connection – Sharon possessed the same animal power and assurance which had coursed through my own father – the hard-fisted, absent womaniser who drove my mother to despair and me, his only son, to hero-worship.

My father could silence a room simply by walking into it. Ariel Sharon wields the same hypnotic charisma.

In the madness of the photo-frenzy, I did not get a chance to speak privately with him. I would like to have reminded him of my prediction, which may have enabled him to save many lives.

But most of all I wish I could have said to him this: 'You have served the God of War well. Now you have a chance which will come to you only once in your life: serve faithfully the Goddess of Peace. The future of the Middle East rests on your shoulders.'

PART 2

Inspirational Encounters

My role, I believe, is as a catalyst. When people meet me or watch me on television, they are inspired by the mysterious feats of MindPower which I demonstrate. Moved to apply their own minds' infinite power to the difficulties in their lives, many people are able to transcend setbacks which had, until then, appeared insuperable.
There are many people who have had this effect on me, and I am profoundly grateful to all of them: Michael Jackson, Bob Dylan, Princess Diana, Muhammad Ali. These are my Inspirational Encounters.

My friend
Michael Jackson

This, I promise, is how you would react if you met Michael Jackson: you'd stare, you'd start, you'd step up and you'd freeze. Everyone does the same thing – fans, celebrities, journalists, children, parents, shoppers, waitresses, prime ministers, prime ministers' bodyguards...

First you look. Michael has the most arresting appearance of any man I ever saw. It isn't only the face, and the clothes. It's the aura. But before you have taken that in, you'll start to move towards him. Instinctively.

You take a step or two, and freeze. It's like being hit by a wave of awareness, first of all pushing you forwards and then stopping you cold in the backwash. 'Oh my God it's Michael Jackson' and then 'Oh! My God. It's Michael Jackson...'

I've been in the massive lobby of an international five-star hotel when Michael walked in, and I've seen the wave sweep over 70 people – not only the super-rich and the professionally cool, but the porters and receptionists and bell-boys. The people nearest him moved, and then froze. Further away, people turned, and moved, and froze, while some of those nearest began to move again. It was like a century-old fragment of celluloid, the lobby suddenly silent and the air flickering, crackling, as people moved in jerks and lurches.

Michael simply smiled and pressed his hands together in greeting.

We drove out of his Knightsbridge hotel in a people-mover with midnight-tinted windows, and there were 2,000 people crowded across the pavement. Around 60 of the younger ones broke from the press and sprinted alongside us. I was concerned that someone could slip and fall under a wheel, but they were all so exuberantly happy. They were shouting out, 'Michael, we love you!'

Michael gestured for the car to slow down, and he edged his door open, leaning out of the car to touch the hands of his fans.

'We love you, Michael!'

'I love you more,' he said. I heard him say it again and again during the next few days. 'I love you more.'

When Michael walks over to a group of fans who have waited hours for a glimpse, you see some of them lock solid. They have messages for him, they want to say how much he has meant to them all through their lives, how his music has been their soundtrack, but all they can do is stare.

Many bring handmade gifts. Embroidered cushions, framed paintings, poems, boxes, candles, national flags. He takes every one and holds it to his chest for a moment. He says, 'Thank you. I love you,' again and again. He does not refuse any request for an autograph or a photograph. I walked with him for 200 yards through the pouring rain across a road in Oxford and past barriers after his address to the privileged Oxford Union audience, to a huddle of drenched and shivering fans. They had not been able to get tickets, and they had turned up on a bitter night without any real hope of being close to Michael for more than a moment, but they (and not the curiosity-hunters in the Union building) were the real fans.

Michael truly loves his fans. When he tells them, he does not do it in the superficial way that most pop stars intend when they shout it from the stage. He means it this way – when Michael walked through the rain that night, he was on crutches, with two broken bones in a foot that was swaddled in bandages. By the time we got back to the limousine he was squeezing filthy, icy rainwater out of the bandages onto newspapers on the floor. I laid my hands on the aching flesh and let energy flow through me, to activate Michael's own healing powers. He sat back with a calm expression on his face and his eyes closed, perfectly accepting of the possibility that healing can begin with positive thinking.

The fan's gifts are displayed in Michael's hotel suites. Wherever he's staying – and he moves around a lot, even between places in the same city – his favourite presents are on display. And he has a lot of favourites. He uses objects almost as pledges, reminders of affection from people who can't be with him, the way you might fill your wallet with photos of your children and folded postcards from old friends. On Michael's walls there are pictures of his own children, of course, and photos of him with his family and friends, but the reverence with which the admirers' gifts are arranged seems to say that his fans are his family too.

I saw how sincerely he felt this when two ingenious German über-fans broke into my home on my wedding day. Michael was to be best man, though by the time the ceremony was due to start neither he nor the rabbi, Shmuley Boteach, had turned up. My manager, Shipi, who is also my brother-in-law, had posted security guards all round the perimeter of the grounds. We were tolerating half a dozen paparazzi who were pointing lenses like cannon barrels over the privet hedge which screens the house from the Thames, and there were a few girls perched in the riverbank trees too, with nothing to see but the marquee and a helicopter. Once or twice the magician David Blaine floated outside for interviews – and I do mean floated. If you haven't yet seen David Blaine levitate then you have a real shock in store.

Many guests commented that I seemed nervous, and I was – but not about getting married. Hanna and I had been together 30 years, and I felt I was probably ready for the commitment. What concerned me was a call from an Israeli source, warning me that there might be a terrorist attack on the wedding. I took the warning very seriously and I engaged all precautions, Scotland Yard referred me to the local police who in turn sent two policemen to discuss the day. Some internationally famous people were there, aside from Michael – the Formula One racing champion Nigel Mansell, Sir David Frost, Dave Stewart of the Eurythmics, the horror writer James Herbert, Dido's producer Youth, not to mention an Israeli consul and the Japanese Ambassador – any terrorist wanting to make a name for himself need only open fire on the canvas walls of the marquee with an automatic weapon. My helicopter pilot was under orders to fly anyone wounded by gunfire to the nearby Royal Berkshire hospital. A medical doctor was on standby, unseen by the guests inside the main house, and Michael's own doctor would accompany him.

Most of the fans, with no thoughts of terrorists, were outside the main gates. A steady stream of guests drove up and announced their names to the guards. The Germans, a boy and a girl, were clever and brazen – they hung around to hear a couple announce themselves, walked away for 20 minutes, then came back and presented themselves under the same names. Shipi saw them walking down our long driveway: 'Who's that?' he demanded nervously, but by then the Germans were inside, and we didn't want a scene. Not in front of the paparazzi. Not on my wedding day. If these guys were willing to behave themselves – and they were – then I decided to be conciliatory, although cautious. They pleaded however to be allowed close enough to say hi to Michael when the ceremony had been concluded.

Michael did more than say hi. He beckoned them to him, embraced each of them gently, accepted their gifts graciously and posed for their cameras. He told them he truly valued their friendship, thanked them for taking such risks to bring him presents, and smiled a blessing upon each of them.

Now, you may be cynical about Michael Jackson. You may be influenced by the highly inventive controversies which have dogged his career. You may be prejudiced by his appearance – though you'd better ask yourself why you feel free to comment on his colour and his looks when you might profess that you never judge anyone by their skin or their face. You may feel that I'm painting him as some kind of saint, when some supermarket tabloids are eager for you to believe the opposite.

I won't bother to argue with you. Michael has maintained the dignity throughout his career to ignore the mudslingers. I know what it is to be falsely accused and reviled, to be laughed at by people who don't have the first idea of what they're saying – but I thank God that the mud aimed at me over the decades has been nothing like the rancid filth hurled at Michael. I have nothing but contempt for some of the people who made such claims, nothing but pity for the people credulous enough to believe them.

All I will say is this: how many other people, now or at any time in history, have possessed the charismatic power to change lives with a smile? To offer a simple thank you and make a person feel deeply, fully blessed?

And how many of those people kept their gift uncorrupted and used it with generosity? There are a few names in your mind perhaps, but I won't make the comparison with Michael. I will leave you to do that for yourself. Let it be a test of how open-minded you can be.

Most people who achieve great fame taste this power, this unexpected gift from God to bestow inspiration on people. Michael has it to an exceptional degree, and this is partly because it has been his to wield for so long. Most sports stars and rock gods lose it after a year or two, as their fame fades. Or they push it away from them without understanding it. Or they foolishly imagine it will protect them from the ravages of their drinking and drug habits. Michael treats the gift with awe, as if it were a healing power which it can be. A smile from Michael can sometimes heal a spirit.

He has an angelic talent for choosing words which will touch the heart. I treasure the inscription on a photograph he gave to me, because he wrote without holding back: 'To Uri, you are truly a Godsend. The world needs you – I need you. Michael'.

When I perform, particularly when I have to bend spoons again and again, I feel drained afterwards. It's not the tiredness that comes from hard labour or long study or too much partying – it's an ennervation, as if I've been sweating raw energy and all my nerve endings are swollen and raw. I often sleep in the back of the car. When he is exhausted, Michael meditates. After the wedding was over and the celebrity photos were all done, he asked me for a room in my home where he could be alone for 20 minutes. Michael is not a frail man, despite what you may have read – he is tall, lithe and his hands are large and strong, like a tennis player's. But at this moment he looked like the finalist after five sets on Wimbledon's centre court. He needed peace of mind.

I showed him into our family room.

Michael's family was famously religious – they were Jehovah's Witnesses and Michael occasionally disguised himself to join his fellow believers as they went from house to house, inviting people to think about God. As a grown man, he has moved beyond denominations of faith – his concern is not with religion but with spirituality. This gives him strength, but I think it is the joy he takes in life which keeps renewing his vitality – that, and a second factor which I shall describe in a moment.

He has a lot of fun, childish fun. Not just child-like, but downright fun. He giggles a lot. He has a great sense of mischief. Michael first became aware of me through reading his school textbooks when he was a teenager. We were introduced by Mohamed Al Fayed, a man whose grasp of English is often variable but whose fluency in swearing is unmatched in any language. Even Hungarians don't swear as enthusiastically as Mo. I think he is spurred on by the presence of people who might be easily offended, like little old ladies or royalty. Or pop royalty – when Mo starts cursing in front of Michael, the tirade is punctuated by delighted giggles and, 'Oh, Mohamed! Ohhhh, Mohamed!'

He loves gadgets. Show him a watch that's calibrated via a satellite link to the atomic clock, or a digital writing pad with a built-in camera, or a mobile phone with a scanner, and he's like a boy – 'That's cool, I love it, can I have it? I mean, just play with it?' He surrounds himself with boyish paraphernalia – pictures of dolphins and sunsets, huge teddies and model cars. He's not into sport much, though he's very fit, like any professional dancer, and he supports newly-promoted Fulham – in the casual way that a lot of teenagers say they support Manchester United, not really understanding the rules or remembering the results, but happy to relate to the team that always wins. Plus, of course, Fulham are owned by a friend of his – Mo took him to a game and they sat there in Fulham scarves and caps. Michael has infinite respect towards Princess Diana who tragically died with Mo's son Dodi whom Michael adored; they were working on a movie together.

Michael's hotel rooms are always decorated with movie posters and eight-foot cardboard cut-outs, Anakin Skywalker peeping out from the folds of Darth Maul's cape, E.T. bicycling over the full moon. The first time I visited him in New York we hired Sony's cinema and took in *The Matrix*, because there's a sequence inspired by me where children teach Keanu Reeves to bend spoons with the power of the mind.

Michael brought popcorn and candy, and his little boy Prince rocketed around between the seats, stopping every few moments to fix me with his luminously intelligent eyes and ask a question. After about half the movie, Michael slipped out of his seat. I didn't say anything and I thought that maybe this was his way of avoiding a 'goodbye' moment. But after four or five minutes I twisted round and saw him, silhouetted under the projectionist's beam. Dancing. Moonwalking to the soundtrack, spaced out in a complex routine of twists and jerks. Anyone could have seen that it was Michael Jackson. No one else on Earth moves that way. Michael Jackson's stunning dance routines in the video for 'You Rock My World' are totally personal to him. This man lives to dance.

He took me to his studio, the Hit Factory – it isn't his own, he merely hires it, but when Michael walks into the recording area it becomes his. He dominates the studio, a different kind of domination to the way he overwhelms a crowd. This is business, and this is the second factor which restores his youth. Michael is utterly committed to his music. He works passionately at it, with a dedication that surprised me when I first saw it. I had deliberately ditched all my preconceptions about this man, because I'd known about his music and his life since I was a young paratrooper and later a paranormalist doing shows for Israeli troops, three decades ago. All that second-hand clutter wasn't going to help me understand the real human being. But in our few meetings and a series of increasingly deep telephone conversations, I had not divined an artist who could be so forceful, so powerful, in the studio.

His attitude shines out of him like an aura. Writing, performing, mixing, arranging – he is in command. Always a confident person who will say what he means even though he says it quietly, in the studio his confidence reaches an entirely different level. He is dominant. And nothing pleases him more than honest praise from another musician. Michael's face was radiant when I told him that Justin Hayward, guru of the Moody Blues, had called me from his home in France especially to tell me to pass a message to Michael. 'You have never made a record that was less than excellent,' he said, 'and this is almost unique among artists of your longevity.'

I think Michael took pride in these words because he knew it to be true. There is not one poor disc. Perhaps not even one poor track. Simply a catalogue of classics. I am proud that Michael liked my own paintings enough to commission a piece of art for the booklet to go with his latest CD *Invincible*. And I was totally flattered when he asked me to energize the tapes which were in the studio's safe.

It wasn't the first time I have worked in this way with super performers.

I visited the Spice Girls in a studio in London around five years ago. They were planning to go to America at the time and before they left I bent a spoon for them and told them to take it to the US to bring them positive energy.

The band were catapulted to success.

I also had a meeting with Elvis once. He requested that we meet about twenty miles outside Las Vegas, saying that he wanted the meeting to be private. He told me to meet him in the desert in a trailer – he was amazing.

At the astonishing party thrown by Michael Jackson to celebrate his 30 years as a solo artist, in New York, I was delighted to spot some youngsters who have achieved extraordinary success since I last ran into them – Joey, Justin, JC, Chris and Lance, the boys of N'sync.

They greeted me as a mentor, which startled me. When we were introduced at a showbiz event in London's Covent Garden, years ago, I had enjoyed their sharp banter and sense of fun, and I'd immediately identified the talent and ambition which could take them to the top – which has made them, in fact, America's biggest pop outfit.

They'd wanted me to bend a spoon, and of course I was happy to oblige. But in New York they reminded me of something else which I had almost forgotten – 'You designed our logo,' exclaimed Justin.

'You grabbed a piece of paper and you drew this five-pointed star, and you told us if we put that star on the cover of our next single and featured it in everything we did, we would be Number One. How did you know that?'

'Did you use the star, then?' I asked, pleased and surprised.

'Did we use it?' they chorused. 'Look at the logo!' And I saw that the jaunty little star was stamped at the left of their name, an acronym made up of a letter from each boy's first name. My drawing is incorporated like an extra letter. On the www.nsync.com website, the stars flash and glitter across their home page.

The five-pointed star has been a powerful symbol of benevolent magic since mankind first began to write. There is no doubt in my mind that the mysterious energies that flow from the pattern have supercharged N'sync's spectacular career.

'Uri, have you any idea how much you should have billed us for?' JC demanded. Over breakfast the next day I told my lawyer the story and he growled, 'Just wait till I hit them with the invoice!'

But I'm very happy to make this a gift to the boys. After all, I couldn't be the fifth Beatle – so I'll style myself as the sixth N'sync instead!

The aftershow party at the Tavern on the Green in Central Park was celebrity heaven. Liza Minnelli gave me a long squeeze and a kiss, and I'm still tingling – I hadn't seen her for years, and she gets sexier and sexier all the time. Marlon Brando looked awesome as he left the stage.

Liz Taylor, though in a wheelchair, is a great beauty. Her presence seems supernatural too, but unlike Brando she is very approachable. 'You have to come down to my home again,' she ordered, 'and unbend all the cutlery from your last visit!'

I had introduced Michael to my friend Rabbi Shmuley Boteach some months prior to this concert, and together we took Michael to a place called the Carlebach Shul in New York for his first visit to a synagogue. We chose this setting because Rabbi Carlebach was famous for his music and his singing. Jewish worship is filled with song, and Michael's face was a picture as he swayed and clapped with the music.

It was during the synagogue service that I began to understand how Michael's gift for bestowing blessings might be most generously spread. Shmuley had the same idea and, as he was moving to New York from Oxford, England, with his wife and six children (it's seven now), the rabbi was able to put his particular gift for practical energy to good use – together, they founded the charity 'Heal The Kids'.

My concept was more abstract. Tormented by the disintegration of the peace process in the Holy Land, I wanted to hold up the aura which emanates from Michael when he is giving happiness to his fans, and shine that like a beacon over Israel. I had no idea how this could possibly be done – I just could not fathom a world where soldiers shot at children who threw stones at cars, and snipers took aim at babies, while millions of people of all races, creed and colour on other continents loved a man who reflected their affection back so dazzlingly. That contradiction just floors me. Everyone in Israel has heard of Michael – his concert a few years ago was a massive sell-out. Everyone would have recognised, at a single glance, his dancing image at the back of that cinema. So what's to prevent his gift of peace from working in Israel?

I remembered a stone I had picked up in the Sinai desert, close to the monastery of St Katerina, when my father and I drove out there one day after the Six Day War. I was recovering from the wounds that I suffered in Ramallah and I believe my dad was proud of me at that time as he never was before or since – my father was a professional soldier. We tried to imagine the place where God had spoken to Moses from the centre of a blazing bush. I sensed I had found the same place at the foot of Mount Sinai – and I can still feel that Moses's foot may have trodden on this triangular piece of rock. We prised it out of the ground and brushed the sand off it, and carried it to the jeep. I told my father its three sides represented Judaism, Christianity and Islam. We drove back to Jerusalem, and close to the Western Wall I placed the stone on the ground. Whenever I returned to the city I went to look at it.

But after the Carlebach Shul, I went back to do more than look. My brother-in-law Shipi persuaded a guard to look the other way while I prised the slab out of the earth for a second time and loaded it into a suitcase. I won't tell you all the difficulties I had getting that suitcase through El Al's security cordon and past US customs, but at one stage I seriously feared the stone would be smashed to shards. Finally, I put it beside me in a yellow cab and called Michael to tell him I was bringing a present. I called it the Stone of Peace. That triangle of rock, I believe, possesses a force which could magnify humanity's potential for peace.

More than a year later, as Shmuley and I posed for photographs with Michael and the Prime Minister of Israel, Ariel Sharon, I realised how we might make the Stone of Peace the cornerstone for our own peace mission. The meeting with Ariel was utterly unexpected. I was staying in New York with a Swiss friend at his Manhattan apartment, when the place was suddenly crawling with security – the kind of security that only Middle Eastern leaders can generate. My friend joked with a bodyguard, 'Who do we have upstairs? Arafat and Sharon?'

'Just Sharon,' came the answer.

Too good a chance to miss. Too good a synchronicity. I believe these strange coincidences are planned for us. And I saw Michael's magic working again. Even the bodyguards moved in stop-start motion. Even the prime minister looked up and reached forward and froze and moved again. I saw the thought written on his face: 'Michael Jackson! That's Michael Jackson!'

I knew then that Michael's gifts could help towards the problems in the Holy Land. We are planning a visit to meet the Israeli president and the Kings of Jordan and Morocco. I have hopes that Arafat too and the leaders of Hizbollah might be willing to sit down with us. We won't expect anyone to negotiate – we are not negotiators or politicians, nor miracle workers. All we can do is hope that music and rhythm and its unifying powers can indeed work a miracle where politics and religious schism fail tragically every day. It is not only we who need this mirage of peace to become real – it is our children, and their unborn children, and all the songs that they will sing.

Muhammad Ali

Ali was my idol. An American who converted to Islam was not an obvious hero to idolise, if you were a young man growing up in Israel. But I knew something about Ali that no one else could see. He floated like a butterfly, he stung like a bee – he thought like a shaman. Muhammad Ali was psychic.

I remember watching footage of the Floyd Patterson fight in a girlfriend's flat in Tel Aviv in 1965. The bout was taking place in Las Vegas and I desperately wanted to be in Vegas. I wouldn't have gambled, I wouldn't even have laid a ringside bet – I simply burned to be in a city with that much energy, watching a fighter with that much power. Ali really punched into my consciousness 18 months later, when he was banned for refusing to be drafted. Uncle Sam wanted Ali to fight the Vietnam War. Ali said, 'I ain't got no quarrel with them Viet Cong,' so the US Army, unable to take Ali, took his world title, his boxing licence and his liberty instead. A few weeks later I was embroiled in the Six Days War. I didn't have a personal quarrel with them Jordan troops neither, but I was already a conscript – refusing the draft was not an option.

When Ali finally got to hit back, KOing a boxer named Jerry Quarry in three rounds in Atlantic City, it was late 1970. I wasn't the only person who could take inspiration from that. Here was a man with the courage to stand by his religious and moral principles, even to the point of ruin. And then here was a man with the toughness to fight all his enemies, and show he could not be beaten. Ali was punching way beyond his weight. He was a heavyweight boxer fighting a million-headed monster – the government, the army, the racists. Beyond that, he looked like a screen idol, he moved like a dancer, and he talked like a street poet.

And I had that one extra reason for worshipping him – he was a natural psychic and knew how to use his powers.

In all his fights, through all the punches he soaked up, Ali never seemed to be hurt. His face was not marked, his bones were not broken. He was living proof of my belief in a protective aura – an energy field generated by the body that repels harm. Any body in good health is exuding this field. Ali did more than exude it – he blasted it out like a 120 decibel vibration. Ali loved to drop his guard and dodge the punches, taunting his opponents. But they had to do more than find the relentlessly weaving target – they had to punch through his invisible barrier.

I wasn't the only one with paranormal theories – in 1976 the *New York Times* published a feature headlined 'Ali's Radar Waves', by Dave Anderson. The next year I got the chance to test them out. A journalist friend was interviewing Ali at his New Jersey training camp. Ali, it transpired, was an amateur magician, and a skilful one. He probably thought my gifts involved sleight of hand, and when he heard I was living an hour away in Manhattan, I was invited to spend a day at the camp. The boxer's entourage would have suited a rock group. There were dozens of people hanging out or just hanging round, waiting for a spark from the champion to flare their way, hoping for advice or endorsements or just plain financial aid. It was worth waiting – Ali was a generous man, with his time and his cash.

I bent a spoon, and he was incredulous. A whole gang crowded around, and even though all eyes were on my hands and the spoon, Ali was the real focus. His charisma picked people up and lifted them through the air – no one could loiter 20 yards away when Ali switched on his extrovert energies. People bristled and leapt into line, like iron filings in a magnetic field. Then Ali did a drawing and I read his mind. It wasn't hard – he had eyes that could penetrate sheet metal. You just had to stand in front of him and his thoughts hit you like 30-foot waves. But when I reproduced a mirror image of Ali's sketch, accurate to one-eighth of an inch, he was stunned. He grabbed my arm and pulled me out of the group. The people around us knew automatically not to follow. As he pushed me around the side of the training ring, the world heavyweight champion's intensity, and his size, were frightening. Sometimes my powers freak people out. Surely Ali could handle it?

He could handle it, and more – he wanted to use this power. He knew he possessed it himself. What he was demanding to know was how to access it. 'I just looked in your eyes and wham, I put a picture in your mind. Can I look in a fighter's eyes and wham, I put defeat in there? Can I make him see how hard he's gonna get hit? Can I knock him out before I ever lay a glove on him?'

We talked for twenty minutes. I told him he was already using his MindPower – when he turned that laser gaze and the brilliance of his charisma on a fighter, the opponent felt weak, like a 40 watt bulb beside a spotlamp. Confusion would kick in and the focus would go. Ali did this instinctively. And more – I believed he was predicting his opponent's moves before a muscle twitched. This wasn't body-reading – Ali was registering the thoughts in the other guy's mind while he was still thinking them. Ali nodded, and turned the idea over. He switched his attention off me, and I suddenly had the alarming sensation that he wasn't there any more. The extrovert energy was shut off. He was internally focused. Staring at his face was weirdly like looking at a Magritte painting of a man who, instead of features, has only blue sky and white clouds.

Muhammad Ali is ripped up by disease today. Most men with his crippling condition would have died years earlier, but the core of that incredible energy still burns inside Ali. I believe disease was already taking its toll in 1978, when he lost to Leon Spinks in the 15th. His psychic strength helped him claim the title back for an unprecedented third time – but it could no longer protect him against every blow. After that fight we knew Ali was not immortal.

Not immortal. Only superhuman.

Peter Sellers

There are many days when, the more I learn, the less I understand. I have been reading a carefully reasoned book which argues that, across the whole infinite expanse of the universe, there is probably no intelligent life except on our planet.

The book is called *Rare Earth*, by two Seattle professors named Peter Ward and Donald Brownlee. The huge timescales needed for 'slime at the bottom of the ocean' to evolve into animal life, the uncommon steadiness of the sun's energy output, the radius of our globe's orbit, the angle of our axis which is governed by a single moon of particular size...change any of these factors and life fizzles out.

'The underlying theme is that the Earth is a charmed place,' Professor Brownlee says. 'We know of no other body which is even remotely like it.'

These facts are easy to follow. They directly contradict what I believe to be true, that there is an intelligence which guides the affairs of man, an intelligence which does not come from Earth. It is extraterrestrial. Call it God, call it aliens – its existence proves there is life throughout the universe.

But that's a matter of faith, and faith usually clashes with science. This isn't hard to understand.

What puzzles me is the cloudy memory of another book.

Probability 1, by Amir Aczel, says it's a mathematical certainty that we are not alone. Applying gamblers' equations to the number of stars in this galaxy and the billions of other galaxies, and factoring in the ease with which carbon-based lifeforms start up, Aczel crunches the numbers and says there has to be intelligent life elsewhere. Any other conclusion is scientific nonsense.

One set of facts, two opposite theories. If I had never read either book, I would have learned far less, and understood at least as much.

It is a great tragedy that, for some people, whole lives can be lived in this ever-diminishing sea of understanding. Information scorches down from every side, and slowly knowledge evaporates.

Peter Sellers, the great comic actor who died over twenty years ago, lived that kind of life. I have always felt a powerful connection to him, perhaps because he could never balance the weirdness of his showbusiness life with his Jewish upbringing. I felt this strongly when I met him in the lobby of the Savoy Hotel in the mid 70s.

For most of his adult life he held a deep spiritual belief which he knew to be true in every detail, though he could not understand it and did not dare discuss it with friends. When he finally explained his experience to the actress Shirley MacLaine, during shooting for his last great movie, *Being There*, Sellers warned her frankly: 'You're going to think I'm bonkers' – and he had driven himself half insane, trying to unravel the truth from the facts.

Peter Sellers had died in 1964. This was a clinically established fact. During the first of eight heart attacks, he told MacLaine: 'I felt myself leave my body. I just floated out of my physical form and I saw them cart my body away to the hospital. I went with it.

'I wasn't frightened or anything like that because I was fine; and it was my body that was in trouble. I looked around myself and I saw an incredibly beautiful bright loving white light above me. I wanted to go to that white light more than anything.

'I've never wanted anything more. I know there was love, real love, on the other side of the light which was attracting me so much. It was kind and loving and I remember thinking, 'That's God'. Then I saw a hand reach through the light. I tried to touch it, to grab onto it, to clasp it so it could sweep me up and pull me through it.'

As the doctors restarted his heart, Sellers heard God's voice tell him, 'It's not time. Go back and finish. It's not time.'

Stories like this were taboo until the mid-Seventies, when Dr Raymond Moody published *Life After Life*. By 1982, a Gallup poll revealed 8 million Americans claimed to have had near-death experiences.

As resuscitation techniques improve, the NDE will become commonplace. Doctors in Tromsö, Norway, revived a woman whose body had been trapped beneath ice for more than two hours. When rescuers pulled her out and began artificial respiration, her body temperature was 23 degrees Centigrade.

The medics patiently kept up an artificial heartbeat for three hours, slowly warming her up – until life returned. Because her mental functions had been literally frozen, the lack of blood and oxygen had not caused any brain damage.

'I'll never fear death again,' Sellers told his wife, Britt

Ekland, after his eighth heart attack. But he did fear life – 'I don't know what it is I'm supposed to do,' he confided in MacLaine, 'or what I came back for.'

The clash between the Jewish culture which shaped him and the film world which swallowed him, between his Jewish religion and his parascientific belief, stripped Peter Sellers of confidence and understanding.

If he had trusted his faith more, and questioned it less... But can I do the same?

Adoption and Beth

Beth has come halfway around the world to be Jewish. She was born in Guangxi, the Chinese province north of Vietnam and came to Britain with an adoption agency.

Her parents were poor city workers who desperately wanted a boy. Chinese law permits a couple to have only one baby, in a campaign to bring the world's biggest population under control. Many baby girls are smothered at birth, human rights workers believe.

Beth was luckier. Her parents gave her up to be adopted abroad. Her new parents are also city workers – Londoners, one a newspaper executive, the other a shia tzu therapist. They already had two boys, and they desperately wanted a girl.

Now Beth has two brothers, one ready for his bar mitzvah this summer and one a PlayStation fiend.

'It's a miracle,' her mother Anat told me. 'Looked at in one way, it seems so impossible – a child from 7,000 miles away, born in a place where most people haven't even heard of

Britain and certainly can't speak English...and her destiny lies here, with us.

'That seems to me so wise, so wonderful, that it can only be an act of God.

'But then so many obstacles, for no real reason, to benefit no one, were set in the path that brought her and us together. Most of the objections have been raised by people who cannot understand that Beth is a human little girl. And that's all she is – she isn't Chinese, she isn't Oriental, she isn't a Communist. She's a girl and she's going to be brought up in London, just like a million other girls.'

Anat and her husband have been tormented by loaded questions and barbed enquiries. Her mother-in-law raised the first objections – was it really fair, she kept asking, to bring a poor little baby all that way and bring it up in a country 'where she'll always be a foreigner?'

'As if there are no other faces like Beth's in London!' snorted Anat. 'What David's mother really means is, "I don't want to have a grand-daughter who looks Chinese." Well, tough. If she's upset, it's her own bigotry that's upsetting her.'

Friends said some strange things. 'You couldn't bring her up Jewish, it wouldn't be natural,' claimed one. 'Who is she going to marry – a white man or a Chinese boy?' asked another, and Anat answered that at six months, there have been no firm proposal of marriage so far.

But the ones who really gave Anat and David the creeps were the professional people – the social workers and the immigration officials. She believes her adoption procedure was shorter than it would have been if the family were taking on a child born in Britain, perhaps one living in a British care home. But there were still many hoops to jump through, and the officials made it flesh-chillingly clear that Anat and David had to prove themselves worthy winners.

'It was like a competition – one wrong answer and we don't

get the prize. And this prize was a human one.'

Social services had Anat's medical file, which showed that her first pregnancy had been fairly straightforward, and the second had nearly killed her. Two gynaecologists both warned that another pregnancy would probably kill both Anat and the unborn child.

They made up their minds to settle for two, and be glad – but the dream of a daughter still lingered. When a colleague told David about the Chinese agency, they decided not to hold back.

'Both the boys have been totally supportive. You'd think they were proof enough that David and I were fit parents,' said Anat. 'After all, if we could have kept on having children, we would have done it years ago, and no red tape could ever have stopped us.

'But these form-fillers came and inspected every corner of our lives. I don't mind divulging our earnings, or our diet – you have to tell these things to tax inspectors and doctors, after all. But some of the questions were totally out of order.

'Did we expect her to observe the Sabbath? What if she wanted to learn about Chinese religion? What if she wanted to eat non-kosher Chinese food?

'Then they insisted on a private interview with the boys, from which we were excluded, and they wanted to know, "How do you feel about having a sister who isn't white? What will your mates think?"'

'I was really proud of their answer – "We don't have a hang-up about race, so why should you?"'

The cycle of form-pushing was broken when David wrote to the head of Social Services, challenging the department to show that his family's Jewishness was not being held against them. Did the officials feel a white Christian family in Britain could adopt a child from China, but a Jewish family could not?

Two days later, approval came through. All the boxes were ticked and counterfoils were signed and dockets were stamped. By the weekend, Beth was in her nursery.

Two centuries ago a baby might be shuttled across a village, from one sister to another, from a mother to a grandmother – now a newborn is whisked around the world, from a family of one race and religion to another quite different, it can even be done via the internet.

But the love is the same. The desire for a child is the same. These are the things that matter most. All loving parents will understand this.

Alyn

There was something extra in Martyn's eye when I crouched beside his wheelchair. His head lolled as he struggled to turn his face to me but his wide brown eyes locked on to mine, and he held my gaze.

'You're looking great,' I told him, and he grinned as he took a deep breath and let out a gutteral sigh: 'Huhhh!'

'He smiled,' I exclaimed to his mother – 'do you think he remembers me?'

'He's pleased to see you, and he says Hi,' Mary said. 'Huh means Hi. He's starting to talk.'

I stared at the four-year-old, pitifully small as he lay strapped in his chair, his legs like chicken-bones poking into a pair of huge, padded black shoes. I tried to smile and I tried not to cry. 'You are so clever, Martyn. You're doing great!'

'Yeah!' said Martyn. I didn't need his mother to translate. For a few moments I couldn't trust myself to say anything, and then I told Mary, 'Martyn's really going to show everyone, isn't he?'

LEFT: With my mother at a year old in the apartment I grew up in in Tel Aviv.

RIGHT: At 11 years old, with my father of whom I was so proud, a few weeks before I left for Cyprus with my mother.

LEFT: At paratrooper training camp in 1966, a year before I was wounded in action.

LEFT: With my mother at one of my first lectures. My mother is related to Sigmund Freud so you can imagine how pleased she was to see me become a lecturer.

BELOW: My first performance at a kibbutz in Israel.

BOTTOM: I endured many secret laboratory tests at Government facilities.

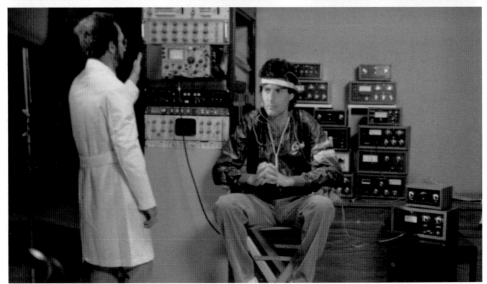

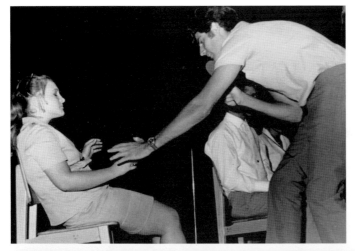

LEFT: To lengthen my performance I began hypnotising people on stage, sometimes in front of an audience of three thousand people.

BELOW: With Salvador Dali, my mentor and teacher who influenced my style of painting.

RIGHT: More laboratory tests, this time at the telementry lab Foch Hospital in Suresnes, France.

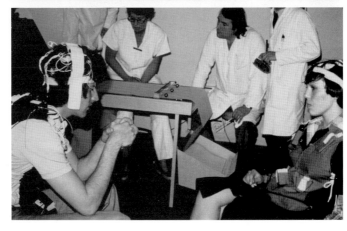

One of my proudest moments was meeting Muhammad Ali. Here we are at training camp in New Jersey in the mid 70s, where I taught him mind techniques.

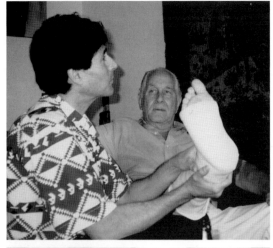

LEFT: With Ronnie Biggs, during his exile in Brazil. I am attempting to heal his broken foot.

LEFT: John Lennon and I talking about UFOs and the paranormal.

BELOW LEFT: David Blaine, the greatest mystifyer in the world, is one of my close friends.

BELOW: Larry Adler, a few days before his death. Larry remained a confirmed sceptic of my powers but was still a good friend.

ABOVE: A meeting with Ariel Sharon, Michael Jackson, Rabbi Shmuley Boteach and myself in New York, 2000.

RIGHT: My children Natalie and Daniel on the day of the renewal of my Jewish wedding vows.

BELOW: Here I am with the Stone of Peace, taken from Mount Sinai and given as a gift by me to Michael Jackson.

BELOW RIGHT: With Michael, my best man on my wedding day.

I bent a spoon for the Spice Girls and told them they would be no.1. Sure enough they were!

With Whoopi Goldberg in LA, 1999.

With N'Sync before they were famous. I designed their now famous logo.

Sarah Ferguson and I at the Royal Academy of Art.

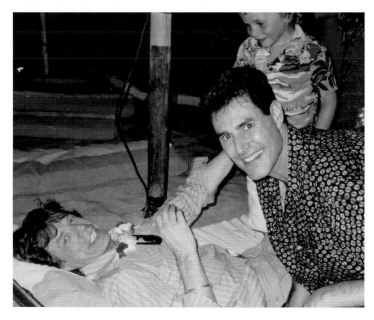

Fooling around with Mick Jagger and his son at Dave Stewart's wedding.

LEFT: Here I am with Destiny's Child and Boris Becker's son, at Michael Jackson's celebratory concert.

BELOW: Sean Lennon, Yoko Ono and I at Michael's concert. Sean found my spoon bending mind boggling.

I didn't know Mary's name until a few weeks before Martyn was born. She and her husband lived near our village, and for years we would occasionally wave to each other on the riverbank, two dog-owners walking their pets. It was always the same remarks – 'Nice morning,' 'Getting colder,' 'Pity about this rain!'

When she was pregnant, a few more remarks were thrown in – 'When's it due?' 'Not long now,' 'Looks like twins!' And I had hoped to see her with a carrypack and a well-swaddled infant, mother and baby walking the dogs. But it was months before we met again, in the post office, and one glance at the baby told me something was wrong. What are the easy remarks then?

Martyn was born with the umbilical cord around his neck. As he travelled head-first down the birth canal, he was slowly being throttled, and by the time the midwife started his breathing, his brain had been starved of oxygen for several minutes. His parents were told he had cerebral palsy and would probably not survive. If he did live, he would be so badly brain-damaged that he could certainly never walk.

He lived, but the doctors never permitted his parents to raise their hopes. They were told to prepare for much hard work, and no reward. Their son's life, the doctors said, would be brief and they should regard that, in some ways, as a blessing.

Perhaps that is what Mary needed to hear. She had to get the strength from somewhere, to train herself up as a good mother – perhaps her fantastic energy flowed from her anger. And she was angry, consumed with fury and defiance at the medics who offered no hope for Martyn.

With her help, he is proving them wrong. I have heard him speak, and it is clear he understands what he hears, and recognises friends he sees. Mary swears she will teach him to read, and I don't doubt it. She aims to help him, somehow, to write, and I know there are ways.

She even dares to hope he will walk – and if anyone possesses the self-belief that can heal a child, it is Martyn's mother.

I returned home that afternoon to find an email invitation from the Alyn Hospital, to address a fundraising dinner in Jerusalem. The Alyn is Israel's only hospital and rehab centre for both Jewish and Arab children with physical disabilities such as cerebral palsy.

I picked up the phone. The meaning could not have been plainer. This was my destiny.

The dinner was sold-out, and 500 guests joined the bidding for a bent spoon which eventually fetched $5,000. I presented an award to a girl of about 14, named Liat, who bravely used her walking frame to cross the room unaided and stand as the room erupted in applause.

I discussed the plight of handicapped children with brilliant therapists and inspiring doctors, dedicated people who are devoting their careers to finding new ways of overcoming impossible odds.

But nothing could prepare me for a vist to the Alyn itself. I have never been in a place of such overwhelming, positive energy, or such devastating suffering.

Of the dozens of children and young people, some were so cruelly paralysed that they could control only their tongues – and yet they had learned to write. Some were born with disabilities, some suffered awful accidents. One child incurred brain damage on an operating table, and the forgiveness shown by her mother humbled me.

All of it was humbling. Until I had been in a place like that, it was impossible even to guess at the depths of human resilience and the immensity of a child's will to learn and heal. Having visited the Alyn, I am aware of how much I will never know about the power of love. Only the children and their parents can ever know.

Rebbe's grave

It is hard to imagine there could be so many prayers in the world. Mountains of prayers, paper mountains. I stood beside the grave of Menachem Mendel Schneerson, known as the Lubavitcher Rebbe, the great Rabbi of the Lubavitcher movement who had recently died. I tore my prayer into fragments, and let them flutter onto the mountain.

Overhead, it was midnight and the landing lights of a 747 thundered on a flightpath to Kennedy airport, less than a mile away. The lips of many of the people there, forty or more, moved as they spoke their prayers aloud, but I could not hear their whispers above the jet's roar.

I found myself wondering if the passengers in the aircraft were touched by the prayers as they floated up. Whether their own prayers for a safe landing were added to the pleas from the holy graveside below...

I had often heard of the Rebbe's grave and the custom of entrusting prayers to his safekeeping. I had not realised how many, how very many prayers there could be, or that they fell in a ragged blizzard on the grave every hour of the day, every day of the year.

'They come by fax,' my friend Rabbi Shmuley Boteach, told me. 'They come by email and they are phoned in, dictated to secretaries. They are sent from every town and city where Jews have settled, and they are being brought personally right this minute. Even as we're sitting here at...' he checked his watch... '10.45pm. We could go there now, get there at midnight, and there would be dozens of people with their prayers, writing them down then tearing them up.'

Naturally I did not quite believe him. And so naturally he had to prove it.

Before we entered the cemetery we saw a billboard, and from the billboard the Rebbe's vast image looked down. Beside his face I read the words, 'Let's welcome Moshiach [Messiah] with acts of goodness and kindness.' Many in the Lubavitch movement he led from the early Fifties until his death in June 1992 believe the Rebbe was the Messiah himself, and that he will return to redeem Israel.

At a Chabad house on the outskirts of the Old Montefiore Cemetery, we joined more than 20 people who had already begun their prayers. One room has been turned into a synagogue, containing a sefer Torah [a scroll of Jewish Law] in a seven-foot steel safe. Videos play of the Rebbe – speaking, smiling, praying, moving with the gentle grace and acceptance of God's will that has struck me in other saintly people: Yehudi Menuhin, for instance, and Dadi Janki.

I watched one screen as the Rebbe handed out hundreds of dollar bills to a congregation, a gesture he often made to remind his followers to give generously and without question.

Stacks of unlined paper were placed all over the house, with bundles of candles. We took a candle each to light beside the grave, and wrote down prayers for kivitlach, for the Rebbe's holy power to intercede with God for us.

The walk is perhaps 100 yards to the mausoleum, and there seemed to be gentiles there as well as Jews. Shmuley whispered that the Rebbe touched so many lives, Reform as well as Orthodox, Christian and Muslim and atheist... especially atheist. It is said that an unbeliever cannot help but weep beside the Rebbe's grave.

We took off our shoes and walked into a stone hut lit by candles. We lit ours too, and approached the burial place of Rabbi Schneerson and the man who was the Lubavitcher Rebbe before him – also named Rabbi Schneerson. Their tombstones were magnificent, but what made me gasp was the truckload of shredded paper mounded over the grave.

The walls around it were three feet high, and the fragments were overflowing. They had been packed down hard, but still thousands were in danger of fluttering over the floor.

'What happens to them? Are they just left there to decompose?' I asked.

'Decompose? The whole cemetery would disappear under paper,' Shmuley replied. 'Every two or three days, the grave is cleared and the prayers are incinerated.'

'And do many people say their prayers are answered?'

'Businessmen. Teachers, Parents. Lovers. Widows. The sick, the old, the guilty, everybody. Even those who don't believe. Especially those who don't believe. So many people have attested to his power – anyone who doubts this is real, they're just deluding themselves.'

Shmuley was getting excitable, and people were starting to recognise him – after his dates on *Larry King* and half the world's other TV shows that year, it would be a surprise to find a Jew who doesn't know his face and his voice. I walked up to the grave and recited my prayer.

Then I tore it in strips and let them fall.

The woman at my side was weeping. I could not hear her, because a 747 plane was overhead, but I saw her shoulders shaking. She was alone. I looked away, and wondered if I should offer a word of comfort.

When I turned back she was smiling. Holding out her hands to the grave and smiling. Then she slipped out of the mausoleum.

And I knew another prayer had been answered.

Suddenly and unexpectedly

Newspapers are part of the Shabbat [Sabbath] ritual in our home. On Saturdays, as on every other day, we have eight or ten of them dropped in a bundle outside the kitchen door.

But on Saturdays, instead of stacking them beside the exercise bike to be speed-read as I churn the pedals at 80kph, I spread them loosely over the oaken table, pour myself a coffee and scan the headlines. Then I start to fillet *The Times*, separating its numerous sections and placing the business, children's and travel supplements to the side, like bones. I neatly tear out two morsels which for three years I have consumed first.

I particularly looked forward to John Morgan's 'Modern Manners' and John Diamond's diary.

This harmless habit has been broken. When John Morgan fell to his death from the fourth-storey window of his rented apartment off Piccadilly. He was 41 years old, and his weekly column on etiquette had never been more popular.

His 'Book of Modern Manners' was in the shops, selling well, and Morgan was becoming a regular on TV and radio. He was on the point of buying a Knightsbridge flat. His brand of playfully old-fashioned advice, for readers who agonised about how to set the places for a dinner party, seemed to amuse everyone, even people like me who would happily wear shorts and trainers to a royal garden party.

Morgan's sheaf of dandy's laws was not snobbish. They were bizarre and fascinating, like the rules of ballroom dancing or synchronised swimming.

John Morgan left no suicide note but his friends say he was prone to sudden fits of intense depression.

I know the building where he lived. My friend, the actor Terence Stamp, had an apartment in the same building. Leaning out of his window on a Sunday afternoon, to enjoy the view of some of London's finest architecture – a view he was planning to leave behind for Knightsbridge – I believe the writer toppled forwards. He died from skull injuries, suggesting a headlong fall rather than a leap.

I have been surprised by how much his death shocked me. Perhaps I felt unconsciously that he was a colleague, since I have been a columnist not only on *The Times* but also for GQ, where Morgan was style editor.

But more than that, the shock stems from the unexpected suddenness of the death. This was clearly a man with an enviable career just waiting to be enjoyed. He had many friends in the media and no rivals – the field was his to take. What a waste.

That same Saturday John Diamond's column was also missing. A footnote said his latest operation on cancerous lumps in his neck had been successful. Sadly, 'successful' for Diamond meant simply that he did not die on the operating table. His disease, which had already robbed him of most of his tongue, was terminal.

For three years he had been charting its progress. At first the prognosis was good – a high percentage of sufferers from that type of cancer survived, he was told.

I remember feeling a chill, which every reader must have shared, at Diamond's own assessment of the odds – 50:50. Either he would live or he wouldn't. Tragically, earlier this year, this brave and witty man finally succumbed.

My biographer Jonathan Margolis and I discussed Diamond's columns a couple of years ago. 'Why is he treating death so trivially?' I asked. 'Why is he still writing about traffic jams and shopping queues? When I meet terminally ill people in hospitals, my thoughts are overwhelmed by how deep life is, and how strong. And those revelations keep the trivia away for days afterwards. Does he live all his life on the surface?'

Jonathan, who knew Diamond professionally, told me, 'John doesn't see himself as an expert on death, or dying. He is still alive, after all. And all the things that filled his life before he was ill, they're the things that still surround him now.'

'He's Jewish, isn't he?' I asked. 'But agnostic. I think he will rediscover his Jewish spirituality.'

Perhaps he did, but he hid it well behind his laconic, mischievous lines. 'Last week,' he wrote in one piece, 'we had an odd dinner party to celebrate Rosh Hashanah with the sort of sometime-Jews who are married to lapsed Catholics and say, '"Remind me again, is Rosh Hashanah the one where they blow that funny trumpet thing, or is that Passover?"'

Because I see very often the real value of our human spirit in healing, I hoped that John Diamond could have found faith in God. I believe that devout prayer can help any disease, and I know that scientific studies are bearing this out.

Recently, for instance, the British Psychological Society heard that positive thinking had a measurable effect on cancer cells. Professor Leslie Walker at Hull University followed 80 women receiving radiotherapy, chemotherapy, surgery and other treatments for breast cancer. Half these women were trained in relaxation and visualisation techniques, using meditation to imagine their bodies fighting back against the disease.

After nine months the positive thinkers all had stronger immune systems. Walker suggests the mindpower practice could have reduced stress levels, making the body more receptive to healing.

John Diamond spent three years showing, inspirationally, how an ordinary life can be lived in the face of oncoming death. John Morgan spent those years demonstrating how to live life with elan and flair.

By sheer accident, the juggernaut has mowed down Morgan. The last, and most trenchant, lesson of Modern Manners is that we all live with the promise of death. And for the correct etiquette in this situation, we must search in our souls.

Saint Edith

Edith Stein knew why she was going to be murdered. As the SS led her from her convent in occupied Holland on 7 August 1942, she told her sister, Rosa: 'Come. We are going on behalf of our people.' Two days later she was killed in one of Auschwitz's four 6000-capacity gas chambers, along with 693 other Catholic Jews.

In her own heart and in the eyes of the Nazis, Edith was a Christian who remained a Jew. When she spoke of 'our people' she was not referring to Catholics. When she was killed it was not solely for warning Pope Pius XII of the impending Holocaust – it was for being born Jewish.

The Pope took his warning, not from her words but from her death. He saw what happened to people who did not fear the Nazis sufficiently, and throughout the war he remained respectfully fearful. There was no disapproval of Nazism at the Vatican until Hitler was dead.

Edith Stein had not been fearful or respectful. The 51-

year-old Carmelite nun who was born in Breslau on 'Yom Kippur' [the Day of Atonement] had united Protestant and Catholic churchmen in protests against the mass deportation of Dutch Jews to the death camps. She had pleaded for an audience at the Vatican – and been refused. She had demanded a papal encyclical, or holy press release, to attack the Nazis – and been refused.

As she called out 'on behalf of our people' to Rosa, Edith Stein knew she was not being persecuted as a Catholic martyr.

But a Catholic martyr is what the Vatican has made her.

Edith Stein has been canonised, declared a saint, in a process which began with her beatification just as recently as 1987. That is quick work, even by the standards of Pope John Paul II, who has created more saints than any of his predecessors this century. A single miracle has been credited to her – the healing of a terminally ill two-year-old in Boston whose mother prayed to Edith Stein. The Vatican is not inclined to go into detail about such things, but it is hard to believe that the mother did nothing except pray to Edith Stein. So the miracle may not be entirely Edith's. For a dying child to regain life is marvellous. For this marvel to be seized upon, and assigned as a Regulation Sanctifying Miracle, leaves a foul taste that disturbs me.

The requirement for miracles is treated like an entrance exam for candidates to the sainthood. Edith Stein was ushered past the examining board like an Oxford undergraduate whose father is an old friend of the Vice-Chancellor.

But it gets worse. Two weeks before Edith got her wings, Alojsije Stepinac, wartime Archbishop of Zagreb, started out to sit the same examination: the Vatican beatified him. Stepinac died under house arrest in Argentina 30 years ago, a convicted Nazi collaborator who allegedly smuggled gold from the teeth of concentration camp victims.

The Vatican says Stepinac was framed by Tito. It also claims he was murdered, by poison slipped into his tea, which means he can be declared a martyr. Stepinac, who fled to Argentina on a Red Cross passport supposedly supplied by Rome, is well on his way to sainthood.

Edith Stein was a convinced Christian, a remarkably intelligent woman whose deep study of theology and philosophy had caused her to renounce Judaism. No one should try to foist her old religion upon her. She died declaring that she wanted to carry the cross of Christ, meaning she wanted to shoulder the sins of the world – including the sins of any Nazis who repented. By her beliefs, she died to save people like Alojsije Stepinac.

But she did not die for the political convenience of the Vatican. Her memory has been manipulated by a world power which failed to protest when millions were being murdered – which failed to protest even when Edith Stein was taken from her convent.

The word 'saint' has somehow become debased. A better word exists for Edith. It is simply 'Good'.

The Book of Ezekiel

One of the publishing sensations of recent years was a reprint. An unknown Edinburgh firm called Canongate took a 400-year-old translation of a 4,000-year-old document, and repackaged extracts in pocket-sized £1 paperbacks.

Sales were sensational. Media interest was unprecedented. The Bible went to No 1 in the bestseller lists.

Canongate's stroke of genius was to commission a 2,000-word introduction for each book from an eminent philosopher or novelist. Louis de Bernières on Job, Will Self on the Revelation of St John the Divine, AS Byatt on the Song of Solomon – the press were thrilled by their unconventional interpretations.

The translation was a Christian one – the King James Bible of 1611. Six books were taken from its Old Testament, six from its New. Only one introduction was supplied by a Jew – David Grossman, Israeli author of *The Yellow Wind*, commented on 'the tempestuous, epic myth of the birth of a nation' – Exodus. The Darwinist Steven Rose, who wrote the foreword for Genesis, although born in a Jewish family, declares at the outset that he has been an atheist since he was eight. All the other writers are, I believe, Christians.

These are the books that formed the Jewish nation. The poetry of Ecclesiastes, the wisdom of Proverbs and the Song of Solomon are the keys to our character. The commentaries Canongate published are relevant and provoking, but these texts are crying out for interpretation by modern Jewish artists, writers, thinkers and politicians.

I would like a Jewish publisher to step forward and repackage the Tanakh [The Hebrew Bible], as a collection of £1 paperbacks, with introductory essays. This concept has already been proven immensely profitable. It could also have a dynamic effect on our culture in Britain, demonstrating in a high-profile fashion that our ancient books are still firing modern Anglo-Jewish thinking.

To give this proposal some weight, I have written a commentary to my own favourite book of scripture, the testament which I believe contains the first record of man's encounters with extra-terrestrial intelligences.

The Book of Ezekiel
You are sitting in darkness. Silence holds you. The entire world is a cinema house, and the sky is its screen. And then a blinding light rips open the screen – not just a projection but a living tornado of flame, blazing through the fabric. The noise around you is the beating of wings, as deafening as a seastorm but filled with the voices of an army. Ten thousand voices, in unison. The sound of God.

And that's just the trailer.

The Book of Ezekiel is the Bible as top-rating TV series – the *Ez Files*. It's about aliens, and sex crime, and the Holocaust. Like a concept for primetime television, it was developed at the height of a ratings war – a religious ratings war, when the one-God-one-faith market leader was seeing its audience share eroded by an explosion of multi-deity cults. Ezekiel staged a fightback so electrifying that even now much of his imagery is too blistering for early evening viewing. He unleashed sudden blasts of horror that have been mankind's recurring nightmares for more than 25 centuries.

A chariot with wheels that are alive, studded with unblinking eyes. The bodies of children, sprawled across shattered pagan altars. A valley strewn with the whitened bones of a whole tribe, which grow flesh and skin, and exist as corpses before the wind breathes life into them. A beautiful woman stripped of her clothes and robbed of her jewels, left to be stoned to death by the men who once lusted for her.

Ezekiel's words are so mystifying and hypnotising it is hard to maintain an objective standpoint. His visions are so lurid and his panting delivery is so urgent, you can feel his hot breath on your face. It takes effort to step back and detach his bony grip, it takes discipline to ask the questions that can put these images in perspective.

- How real are Ezekiel's visions of angels and machines?
- Why does he rage about whores and harlots with such fervour?
- What is the meaning of his horrific visions of slaughter and mass graves?

The book opens with a vision of God which tallies in many respects with modern accounts of UFO encounters and abduction by aliens. Ezekiel is a priest among the Israelite slaves in Babylon when God appears to him, on a chariot drawn by four humanoid creatures. 'Every one had four faces, and every one had four wings' (Ez 1: 6). From one direction they had men's faces, from another the heads of lions, from another oxen and from another eagles. These are the four essences in Middle Eastern mythology – the original earth, wind, fire and water. To an audience tempted by animal gods and fire worship, Ezekiel's angels would have been instantly convincing. The question is – did Ezekiel create the image consciously, or subconsciously...or was it created for him? And if the last answer is the right one, who was the creator?

I do not believe any imagination, and especially not Ezekiel's, could invent these visions deliberately. Every detail is inspired. They resonate with images found in astrology, alchemy, Tarot and the mythologies of all continents. Native North Americans, Vikings, Aborigines and Bushmen would understand the symbolism. But for most of the book, Ezekiel's language is plain. He is fiery, but he sticks to the facts and the storylines. Nowhere in all his 48 chapters does he achieve the aching, rending beauty of a single line from Ecclesiastes. This is not the language of a creative genius.

It is more plausible to say Ezekiel's angels sprang from his unconscious. This is a very vague plausibility – not exactly meaningless, but able to be moulded into almost any meaning required. On the brink of the third millennium, a vast swathe of the human mind is unmapped. We don't know what goes on in the parts that think in pictures, not words. Carl Jung theorised that we all share an unconscious mind, like an image library we can plunder for metaphors to explain our existence. This must be at least partly true, if we are to understand why the four-headed monsters that thrilled the exiled Israelites can instantly grip readers today with horror – post-Gulags, post-Hiroshima, post-Final Solution, post-everything so much more horrific than a four-faced freak from Scripture.

Temporal lobe seizures have been identified by neuroscientists as the root of some religious visions. Positron

Emission Tomography scans can identify which areas of the brain are active during particular functions – one zone of the cerebral cortex, above the forehead, plays a crucial role in both visionary experiences and epileptic fits. By stimulating this region, labelled the God Spot, neurologists have induced states of religious ecstasy in some epileptics. This theory certainly fits observations of some saints and mystics, such as the Franciscan monk St Joseph of Copertino, who could be plunged into trance simply by the mention of a holy word.

But if Ezekiel's vision was caused by a brain malfunction, and fed by the common psyche, how can its modern aspects be explained? In verse after verse, events are detailed that match the stories told by tens of thousands of people in the 1990s. People who remember abduction by unknown, alien beings are talking about a very similar kind of vision, in a very different context.

Sightings of spacecraft have been recorded for centuries. Ezekiel is not the only Biblical prophet who may have seen a UFO – Elijah's fire from heaven, described in 1 Kings, also fits the pattern. In modern Israel, south of Haifa, there is a hollow in a cliff known as Elijah's cave, and some ancient painter has depicted a distorted disc. On the Mediterranean shoreline below, Shikmona Beach has been the scene of several well-documented UFO sightings, including one which left a distorted disc identical to Elijah's burned onto the sands.

The idea of visitors from other parts of the universe is a new one, though, and UFO studies are barely 50 years old. Abduction is an even newer phenomenon – the first serious discussion began in the Eighties, and it was not until the massive advertising campaign for Whitley Strieber's *Communion* in 1987 that it gained wide notice. Whatever the truth of the stories – and most abductees find it very hard to believe their own memories can be anything but a delusion –

there are many common elements. These make alien abduction a much more interesting phenomenon than simply spotting UFOs. Thousands of separate descriptions speak of messengers who seem to glide without moving, who turn without facing a different direction, and of spaceships like immense crystals. Abductees are lifted head-first, pulled upwards by an unseen force, and the scenes of their abduction tumble one after another without connecting sequences – abductees may remember a dozen different rooms, but never how they were transported between them.

Ezekiel's angels move thus: 'They went every one straight forward: whither the spirit was to go, they went; and they turned not when they went.' Or, as the JPS translation says, 'Each could move in the direction of any of its faces; they went wherever the spirit impelled them to go, without turning when they moved' (Ez 1:12). The throne of God – or the mothership – 'was as the colour of the terrible crystal, stretched forth over their heads above' (Ez 1:22). Ezekiel is addressed, on 87 occasions, as 'son of man', a phrase which could almost mean 'Earthling'. It is scarcely used anywhere else in the Bible.

In the second of the prophet's four visions, God 'put forth the form of an hand, and took me by a lock of mine head; and the spirit lifted me up between the earth and heaven'. Ezekiel is brought to a series of gates and doors – the entrance to Jerusalem, and to its temple, and then the inner sanctum and the altar, and finally to the city's higher gate, where six avenging angels are arrayed. At each new door he arrives effortlessly, magically. The messages he receives are warnings of worldwide cataclysm and Armageddon, which abductees today often echo. And which very much resemble the state of our planet today, threatened by terrorists.

If Ezekiel's vision was an eruption of his unconscious mind, then this mental phenomenon has been secretly occuring for at least 2,500 years. If it involved an outside intelligence, then abduction is a terror which has been with us in all cultures, throughout history. And if it was a true manifestation of God – then up to one million people in America alone may have come face to face with God in the past decade.

I have long believed that God is unseeable and unknowable. He showed himself to Moses through a crack in the rocks, and a glimpse of the hem of his robe was dazzling. He spoke, like the voice of an army, to Ezekiel. But God has never stood bare and all-powerful before any man. If he did, he would be simply incomprehensible.

Instead, I believe, there are intermediaries. Messengers, emissaries. Intelligent powers. We called them angels, and when we stopped believing in angels, we called them aliens. As the descriptions of Ezekiel show, aliens and angels are the same thing.

To hear Ezekiel preach must have been an extraordinary revelation. He was a supremely dramatic performer. I believe he really was struck dumb (Ez 3:26), probably by psychological shock – but the business of lying down for weeks (Ez 4:04-4:07) is pure theatre. He might as well have chained himself to the railings. In his most mesmerising performance (Ez 5:01), Ezekiel shaves his head and beard – he was a big man, and shaven bald must have been as imposing as a heavyweight boxer. He chops the hair into three portions and destroys one by fire, one by the knife and one by scattering it to the wind – the fate God promises for the Jews.

For more than 100 searing verses (Ez 16, 23) the prophet talks of sex. He accuses his people of behaving like an ungrateful, unfaithful wife. Jerusalem was a lost little girl when God adopted her – when she was grown he made her his wife, but she rewarded him by giving herself to every other god within a radius of 500 miles. She deserves every punishment possible, and she's going to get it. Ezekiel is in a lather of righteous excitement as he paints the woman's lewdness and humiliation. Why is this written in such scalding detail?

Israel and Judah are sisters who become whores in Egypt, and strive to outdo each other in perversion and depravity. Their craving is for the beautiful boys of the Assyrian army, 'clothed in blue, clothed most gorgeously, horsemen riding upon horses, all of them desirable young men...whose issue is like the issue of horses'. Why is the prophet flaying himself, and his audience, into this frenzy?

I believe the Book of Ezekiel was recorded as a picture of the most mesmerising preacher in the world at work. The material has been chosen, not to provide a structured message, but to preserve his greatest sermons. These two, with their whores and idols, their rapes and slayings and their strutting soldiers, with their fire and brimstone and terrible judgments, must have had the crowds on their knees and panting for more.

Every advertising executive knows it now, but Ezekiel knew it 500 years before Caesar was born – sex sells.

The prophecies fall into a different category. There are images of death here, which are not parables. The visions of slaughter were not recounted to teach, but to tell. These are what Ezekiel was shown by God, and these are what came to pass. He saw destroying angels like Nazi stormtroopers, ordered to put the Jews to death (Ez 9). A scribe is sent through Jerusalem, marking the foreheads of the pure and so condemning the others to massacre. Six executioners, 'every man a slaughter weapon in his hand,' are ordered to follow the scribe through the city, 'and smite: let not your eye spare, neither have ye pity: Slay utterly old and young, both maids, and little children, and women: but come not near any man who has the mark; and begin at my sanctuary. Then they began at the ancient men which were before the house. And he said unto them, Defile the house, and fill the courts with the slain: go ye forth. And they went forth, and slew in the city.'

There is no more clinical description of the events in the ghettos of Warsaw and Lvov in May 1942. The racially pure were marked out – by the scribe's ink, not on their forehead, but on their birth certificates. The weapons of slaughter in the hands of men were guided by the scribe, who saw to it a star was worn by every human being condemned to destruction. First the elders were slain, beginning at the house of God. Then every house was defiled, and the courtyards were piled high with the slain, and there was no pity. The maids died, and the little children died.

The Book of Ezekiel is lurid and brutal. It is not an 'enlightened' text but then we are living through a lurid and brutal era. And all our 'enlightened' texts have not been much use.

Bible code

Here's a conundrum for Bible scholars: identify these verses from the Book of Ezekiel. 'New York: They accompany the unfortunate who are stricken in it. The worshippers are gathering around God.'

These lines come from Ezekiel 7, though you will not recognise them – the words are formed by an extended sequence of letters, occuring at regular intervals. The system, developed by Professor Elyahu Rips of Hebrew University, has been dubbed the Bible Code.

Rips's computer programme scans the Tanakh for 'equidistant letter sequences' (ELS) to find clusters of words embedded, or encoded, within the text. For instance, the word 'LOVE' is spelled out at regular intervals in the phrase 'aLl of Our aVenuEs'.

Here the skip, or interval between key letters, is just four characters. The chances of such a sequence appearing somewhere in the Bible are very high – at this level, finding small hidden words is no more than an amusing game.

You might even play it with this article: for instance, I just unintentionally encoded the word 'NOW' at three letter intervals by including the phrase 'appeariNg sOmeWhere'.

To find single syllable words is unsurprising. To find two entire sentences, comprising 17 words, with an unvarying skip of 15 letters, is utterly mind-boggling.

But to discover that the sentences hold both a prediction of and a verdict upon the atrocity of 11 September is unimaginable. It leaves no room for doubt that the message must have been directly injected into the text by its author.

Ezekiel was only the scribe of his Book, of course. Its author, by divine inspiration, was God Himself.

The Ezekiel cluster was decoded from the Hebrew text, discovered in the early verses of Chapter Seven where the prophet warns, 'Thus said the Lord God to the land of Israel: Doom! Doom is coming upon the four corners of the land. Now doom is upon you! I will let loose my anger upon you and judge you according to your ways. I will show you no pity and no compassion.'

The dreadful consonance between the two messages, overt and hidden, makes both more dreadful.

The decoding work is being done by author and mathematician Edwin Sherman, director of the Bible Code Digest. He is also working on many short ELS which appear to be prophetic of the catastrophe, including 'Repent! God has responded to the evil,' and 'An unheard-of disaster.' By arranging the letters in a grid, so that the program can compile ELS by skipping vertically through the holy text as well as along the lines, Sherman has also discovered the '11 September' and '2001' cross each other at one point.

Crosses such as this are believed to be intensely significant. When the atheist Bible Code scholar Michael Drosnin began to investigate Professor Rips work in 1994, he was horrified to learn that the only time Yitzhak Rabin's name appeared in full as an ELS, it was crossed with the phrase, 'Assassin that will assassinate'. In November 1995, Rabin was gunned down.

Skeptics have tried to debunk the code, claiming that ELS will appear in any major text. But their researches have proved precisely the opposite. One brief, seven letter Jewish holy word – Hanukah – was unearthed in a translation of Tolstoy's *War And Peace*, but the odds against such a small discovery were pretty low, about 1 in 5.

In other words, chance dictated that, if the skeptics hadn't found what they were looking for in *War and Peace*, it would have been there in *Anna Karenina*, or *Moby Dick*, or *Middlemarch*, or *The Way We Live Now*.

On the other hand, the odds against an ELS like the 22-letter message embedded in Isaiah 53 are too vast to be understood – 1 in 8.3 to the power of 99. That's 83 followed by 98 zeroes. I could fill the rest of this page just by writing it out. Sherman compares the skeptics findings to the Biblical ELS as 'a pile of sand next to Mount Everest.'

And the improbability of the Ezekiel cluster is still more horrific.

Elyahu Rips did not invent the concept of a Bible Code. It has been known in mystical Jewish tradition throughout our history. Before the Torah was ever written down, rabbis understood that it was, literally, the word of God and that no changes must ever be introduced. By the 12th century, when scribes were working constantly to copy Tanakh manuscripts, the rabbis would warn that a single slip of the pen could irrevocably alter a text and, consequently, bring about the end of the world.

The Slovakian rabbi Michael Ber Weissmandl, who escaped from a Nazi death train during the war and fled to America, studied the writings of scholars who had broken fragments of the code. But Weissmandl, unlike the Enigma code-breakers at Bletchley Park who ended German naval supremacy by solving their codes, had not even rudimentary computers to help him.

Rips teamed up with a physics graduate, Doron Witztum, and a young programming genius, Yoav Rosenberg, to unravel ELS which could have skips of many thousands of letters, with pages of text occuring between each key letter. They made the Torah circular, so that it's last letter was followed by its first and the ELS could revolve endlessly.

The research is arduous because, unlike at Bletchley Park where German transmissions were intercepted every day as a starting point for code-breaking, the Bible decoders have no hints. Trial and error is the only way forward, with likely words and every possible skip painstakingly investigated.

Sherman likens it to hunting for fossils by randomly digging holes in the ground, until a dinosaur is found. He also notes that the initials WTC occur far less often than chance would predict – as if the sequence for World Trade Center was a troubling gap on the landscape.

Even with such work-intensive systems, the code-breakers have found incredible evidence of hidden prophecies. As Sherman says, 'One can only wonder if Nostradamus has been seriously upstaged.'

Sinai icons

It was a face that might be seen on any London street today – an old man's face, scored with the anguish of poverty and sickness. His hair was long and matted, his beard was straggling and dirty.

In his rags and frayed sandals he seemed to mock the opulence all around him – the well-dressed, well-fed people who moved among the antique furnishings.

Beside him stood a young man – his son perhaps, until I looked more closely. The youth had an earnest, idealistic face, but his clothes were of the same battered material.

A carrion bird hovered close by. It looked as if it might expect one of us to throw a handful of crusts at the old man's feet. If a crumb dropped, the bird was ready to swoop.

My hand reached instinctively to my pocket for spare change. I stopped the ridiculous gesture.

This creature was not a beggar. He was a holy man. A prophet. And he had been dead for thousands of years.

I was standing before an eleventh century painting of the Prophet Elijah. And if you doubt my story, if you do not believe that a medieval work of art can provoke such a modern reaction, then I urge you to visit the exhibition of Byzantine icons from the Monastery of St Catherine at Mount Sinai.

The Prophet Elijah Fed by a Raven was painted by an artist known only as Stephanos, around 1200 CE. It symbolises a prayer for forgiveness, Elijah clasps his hands in supplication, and the hand of God appears in answer to the prayer.

It once decorated the Elijah Chapel on the path to the summit of Mount Sinai. The ascent beyond the monastery can only be achieved on foot. Generations of monks have hewn 3,750 steps into the Sinai stone, from St Catherine's to an ampitheatre known as the Seven Elders of Israel. From the Seven Elders 750 steps rise further, to the Chapel of the Holy Trinity on the very peak of the mountain.

The younger man is Moses. Again this icon is a prayer for God's forgiveness by Stephanos; an inscription over the Burning Bush is a prayer for the soul of a man, or a boy, named Manuel.

Moses reverentially holds the tablets bearing the Ten Commandments. He has removed his sandals to stand on the holy ground, the same piece of mountainside where the Moses Chapel was built and where this icon hung for centuries.

Until a recent London exhibition, entitled 'Sinai, Byzantium, Russia,' neither artwork had ever left the monastery. They were on display with 18 other pieces. Seven have never been seen outside St Catherine's. One, an icon of St Nicholas, has been exhibited previously, and the remaining ten are key works from the holdings of the State Hermitage Museum, St Petersburg.

Almost all are clearly Christian pieces. The depiction of

the 12 stages of martyrdom of St Catherine. for instance, impresses and fascinates me as an 800-year-old work of devotion and spirituality, but I feel no kinship with the Christian saint.

Sinai is a powerful symbol in my spiritual heritage, though I do not share the beliefs of the monks.

The paintings of Elijah and Moses struck me in a very different way to the other icons. These two men are, with Abraham, the founders of my faith. They stood austere and aloof from the saints, apostles and martyrs – I had a sense that I had discovered my father and my grandfather among a glittering reunion of my distant cousins.

To see these men in relation to the overtly Christian icons was a stark reminder that the Jewish faith is far more ancient than any other. It was to the Jews that God spoke in the desert, so many millennia ago.

St Catherine's, though its monks worship Jesus, is an enduring memorial to the original faith, the religion which literally set down the spiritual laws which still guide us today. The cornerstone of the monastery is a Jewish rock.

Its collection of icons is one hundred times larger than this exhibition – there are 2,000 artworks there. The library holds twice as many unique and ancient manuscripts.

One is the Chrysobull of Mikhail, Tsar of Russia, a parchment dating to 1630. It describes itself as an imperial charter to the abbot of Sinai or his successors and the brethren of the monastery 'of the most holy Mother of God of the Burning Bush'.

This document replaces an earlier one which was stolen when an abbot was killed on the road. It grants the right to travel to Moscow every four years, free of charge, to raise alms and financial assistance for building work.

In a time when all reporting of the religious and political conflict in the Holy Land speaks as though the history of

Israel began in 1948, this exhibition reveals an overpowering truth – all man's spiritual beliefs interlock at Mount Sinai. Israel is as old as Elijah. Neither Christianity nor Islam – for the mountain is a holy place to Muslims also – could have existed without the Jews.

When the exhibition closed, many of these artworks were returned to St Petersburg, a city formerly known as Leningrad.

The word 'Leningrad' appears nowhere in the exhibition. The recent miseries of Communism in Russia are no longer relevant, a forgotten sickness.

I pray that the hatred between religions which have riven the Holy Land and now the world will be wiped away as swiftly.

Larry Adler

Larry Adler told me, more than once, how he made up a tennis foursome in Hollywood in the Thirties, partnering Salvador Dali against Charlie Chaplin and Greta Garbo. It's the ultimate anecdote and Larry knew it. The world's greatest comic, its most glamorous femme fatale, one of its most brilliant artists...and a Jewish guy from Maryland with two tons of chutzpah and a mouth organ.

Larry insisted it was a mouth organ. 'I don't play the harmonica,' he said, drawling the word with distaste. He converted serious composers to the instrument: Ralph Vaughan Williams wrote Romance for Mouth Organ, Piano and Strings for him; Gershwin said he made 'Rhapsody in Blue' sound like it was written for a mouth organ.

I loved bumping into him, because he was full of surprises – even though the best anecdotes might have been heard before (and I'll recount the one about the gangster and the Sabbath in a moment) Larry was always fizzing with memories and energy.

And I admired his defiant spirit. This was an artiste who, when he had elbowed his way into the Peabody Conservatory of Music in Baltimore, was expelled after a perceived slur on his Jewishness – at an end-of-term concert, one of the teachers asked, 'What are we going to play, little man?'

Adler was seething, and ditched his plan to perform Greig's Waltz in A Minor. Instead, he chose 'Yes, We Have No Bananas.'

As a boy in Maryland, discrimination was everywhere. 'Everyone hated everyone else,' he said. 'I was called a 'Jew bastard' on my first day at school, and warned by my parents not to play with 'the little nigger boys'. So I went out of my way to play with them.'

The same furious principles got him kicked out of the US during the McCarthy witch-hunts of the Fifties. Adler was no Communist: he had simply backed Humphrey Bogart's Committee for the First Amendment, protesting against the blacklisting of left-wing Hollywood writers. The House of Representatives UnAmerican Activities Committee investigated them both – Bogart, the screen's biggest idol, barely survived, and Adler was exiled for 20 years. In the Eighties he was one of those brave enough to support Salman Rushdie by joining in a public reading of *The Satanic Verses*.

It's ludicrous to imagine that anything Larry did could be called unamerican. He created himself as a star and a great musician, from a small-town upbringing, and he partied with the most glamorous people on the planet while he philandered his way through a succession of beautiful women, a few of whom he married. What could be more essentially American?

He discovered in middle life, he told me, that the family name wasn't Adler but Zelakovitch. His Russian-born grandfather, fed up with being alphabetically at the back of every queue with a name no one could pronounce, leap-frogged to the front. Larry Zelakovitch would probably have been just as musical, but the new name was sharp and quickfire, like his trademark demi-semi-quavers.

Larry was the youngest cantor in a Baltimore synagogue by the time he was ten, but in later years his Jewishness was all about culture rather than religion: he became an unshakeable atheist.

At his memorial service at Golders Green crematorium's chapel, there were no religious observances. That was his wish, and his friends and family respected it.

I tried to make him appreciate the existence of a more profound reality than our own, but he waved all talk of the mind's powers aside with a spluttered 'Pah!' Every time we met, I bent a spoon for him, sensing that he was an acute and intelligent man who would not deny the evidence of his own eyes.

Larry always turned away at the instant the spoon began to bend, refusing to witness the mystery. 'Have you been brainwashed by sceptics?' I snapped at him once, and he just dismissed the whole subject with another explosion of 'Pah!'

He was very sick when we last met, just a few days before his death on 7 August 2001 from pneumonia at St Thomas's Hospital, London. He told me he had had two strokes and had been treated for cancer. Yet his intellect and his memory were undimmed, and he was happy to reminisce for as long as he had an audience.

I believe he is reminiscing still. Despite Larry's atheism, I am convinced that his spirit has outlived his death. He's probably pretty shocked about it, and secretly pleased. I do not understand exactly what happens to any spirit after we die, beyond my certainty that all of us will survive, but I do think that people who denied their spirituality throughout their lives will embrace the idea in death.

Oh yes – that story about the gangster. At a Chicago party on a Friday night, an aggressive man told Larry: 'What kind of Yid are you? Get your coat, go back to your hotel, sit down and write your mother and father a letter. And this Saturday, I don't give a damn how many shows you got to do, you're going to synagogue like a good Jewish boy.'

Larry did. I asked why, and he said, 'You didn't argue with Al Capone.'

Bob Dylan

It's hard to find what you want when you don't know what you're looking for, and last night I was sitting in front of my computer screen with only a vague notion of what I was seeking. Something odd, something entertaining, something unique – some bizarre site for my weekly Weird Web column in *The Times*.

I'd been browsing since 10pm, and now it was past 2am. I'd found a lot, but not what I needed, and my wife Hanna had long gone to bed. To keep myself company, I slipped a CD into the machine.

I chose Bob Dylan's *Blood on the Tracks*, because it had been delivered that morning from an online music store. The first time I bought it was in a Greenwich Village store in 1975 – I don't use my vinyl records much now, because it's hard to play a $33^1/_3$ RPM disc on a computer. Gradually I'm replacing my favourites.

As I studied the track listing, I realised this album was only half a favourite. I don't ever remember playing the second side of the record. I wore out the first side – I know the lines of 'Tangled Up In Blue' and 'Simple Twist Of Fate' like a child knows prayers and nursery rhymes, almost like an instinct. But that first side seemed a complete work of art, and I never flipped it over.

A CD has no second side. And as I kept clicking and searching in the Web, the familiar music ran out and songs I did not know began to play.

The last track was a revelation. It pulled me out of my virtual world, and I sat back in the flickering darkness of my study, and played that song over and over.

It is called 'Buckets Of Rain', and it sounds like a traditional folk song, and it also sounds very Seventies, like Cat Stevens. It has a loose, live feel, and a lyric which seemed to sum up all the friendships which have ebbed and flowed since I lived in New York a quarter of a century ago – and how my wife Hanna has always been my rock.

When Dylan became a Christian evangelist in the late Seventies, one fan I knew, an accountant in LA, threw out all his albums. He had everything the singer had released since 1961, some of it autographed, and he heaved the whole collection into a skip. I told this man, Milton, he was acting like the Bible Belt fundamentalists had when they burned Beatles LPs in protest at John Lennon's 'we're bigger than Jesus' ad-lib.

Milt wrote to me, 'How can I ever listen to Dylan's stuff again? I've always loved it, it's been the score of my whole adult life – student days, meeting my first wife, hippy peace marches, raising a family with Judith, then that divorce...I did it all to the sound of Dylan.

'But now that man, my idol, who was born a Jew named Robert Zimmerman, is walking onto rock and roll stages and proclaiming, "Christ will return to set up his kingdom in

Jerusalem! There really is a slow train coming and it is picking up speed! Satan has been defeated by the cross!"'

'It's a betrayal. I feel tainted with hypocrisy. Dylan talked about emigrating to Israel – he went there repeatedly, he spent time on a kibbutz, he was photographed at the Wall. It's like finding out someone you love has been lying to you all their life. I have to deal with that, and dealing with it means dumping the records. That's not a protest, it's a defense mechanism.'

Rereading Milt's letter has made me think hard about what fans can expect from their heroes. Dylan did not write his songs as a soundtrack for Milt's adventures – he wrote them for himself. So it was unreasonable of Milt to hold his idol to his personal code of conduct.

I believe Milt could have kept listening to *Blonde on Blonde* and *Freewheelin'*, without turning Christian – and without the right to insist that Dylan stayed a Jew.

Frederic Chopin was an anti-Semite, and that doesn't prevent me from loving the Nocturnes and Waltzes. I don't hear a Jew-hater when I listen to the Ballade for Piano No 1, and I don't hear a fire-and-brimstone evangelist when I listen to 'Hey Mr Tambourine Man'.

In the mid Eighties, Dylan was reportedly interested in Hasidic Judaism and the Lubavitch movement. I don't hear that either in the songs I have just discovered in *Blood on the Tracks*. What I hear, as Milt heard, are the echoes of my own life. If I was a Buddhist, or a Moslem, these would be Zen songs or Islamic songs. But I am Uri Geller – and right now, 'Buckets of Rain' is a uniquely Uri Geller song.

Now if Diana had been Jewish . . .

She was always the fairytale princess, and fairytales are vicious stories, full of curses and misery and bloodshed. Perhaps we should have expected her to die.

But when it happened, the world was so terribly shocked that our reactions became a bigger issue than her death.

I heard the news on CNN, very early on the Sunday morning, in the gym of a Berlin hotel. The previous night I had recorded a light-hearted TV show, and I was planning to take the family shopping after breakfast. I have to bicycle hard for 50 or 60 minutes, to damp down my energy levels, first thing in the day. At home, I write while I cycle, but in Berlin I didn't have my specially adapted machine. So I watched TV.

I'm telling you this to emphasise the mundanity of it. I was in an anonymous hotel. I wasn't doing anything special at that minute, and I wasn't planning anything special for the whole day. But I can recall everything about 6.15am

European Time on 31 August, as if it happened an hour and not a few years ago. The sports shirt I was wearing, the squeak in the right pedal of my bike, the wary, disbelieving tone in the newscaster's voice as she relayed first that Diana had been seriously injured in a car crash in Paris, and then second – that Diana was dead.

The roomful of books published about her since then have interpreted the fairytale in every possible light. Andrew Morton made her death the tragically inevitable consequence of a royal soap opera, like the demise of Bobby Ewing in Dallas. One of the weird qualities of grief is to make everything unreal, and half the world believed, like Morton, that the twisting plotlines dreamed up by Buckingham Palace would eventually mean Diana would be written back into the story.

Internet conspiracists agreed – the crash was a mock-up, engineered by the super-rich Fayeds, to give the young lovers freedom from the ever-watching world. Or it was a secret service murder – Diana, the central character was being dropped because the actress had become too demanding.

As the soap washed off, the psychologists stepped in. Diana was claimed as an icon for the Freudians, the Jungians, the nihilists, the New Agers, the post-moderns, the post-feminists, the far Left, the far Right, the monarchists and the anarchists. Books with titles like *Deconstructing Diana* and *The Id and Di* claimed her as a sexual liberator, a victim of food fascism, a media manipulator and a paparazzi puppet. In the hands of her brother she became a weapon, as he stood in the Abbey and seemed to take arms against her estranged in-laws. In the eyes of mourners who laid 10,000 tons of flowers at Kensington Palace, she was simply a saviour.

In Britain, the predominately Christian media have struggled with this multi-faceted icon. A saviour who dies without absolving her own sins? The virgin mother of the future King, who has a succession of brutally painful love affairs? She is a muddle of sin and saintliness and sex and celibacy. Diana, even as a goddess, is a very different kind of goddess to Mary.

Years later the world is much more confused about its fairytale princess than ever it was when she was alive.

And yet I don't feel confused. All the talk of ritual significance and religious symbolism sounds like a foreign language. To me, Diana was a woman and a mother. To her children – to all children, in fact – she behaved as a good mother. To her husband, and her lovers (including the press), she behaved as a capricious woman. Is that hard to understand?

Perhaps this is a Jewish perspective. The Jews abandoned all worship of goddesses when Moses brought the tablets down from Mount Sinai. We don't expect women to achieve transcendent holiness, just because they want to help sick youngsters. The God of the Jews is male. The women of the Jews are noble and inspiring – Judith and Ruth, Esther and Bathsheba. They are not icons or saviours. To make them into goddesses would be a sin against God.

This is the great strength of Jewishness – it's simplicity. Men are men and women are women. There are good acts and bad deeds. There is love and family and faith and prayer. We are all equal, and the impossible is expected of no-one.

If Diana had been treated as a woman and not a myth, a girl and not a goddess, we would have understood her a great deal better. And perhaps hounded her less. Now if Diana had been Jewish...

But that, of course, would have been quite impossible.

Steven Berkoff

I have dedicated my career to spreading positive energy, to enthusing people about the hidden potential of the human mind and preaching the value of love above all emotions. But the actor/director Steven Berkoff saw me as Satan. At a recent meeting this hypnotic man stared at me as he gripped my hand and said, 'You must play Satan for me.'

And I wanted to say yes.

Berkoff's latest play is *Messiah*, a brilliant retelling of the death of Jesus. It opened at the Edinburgh festival last year but was denied a proper West End run and is now touring the country with a breathtaking cast.

Berkoff's belief is that Jesus may not have been the Son of God but he was certainly the Father of PR. Crucifixion created a legend, and the disciples were his spin-doctors.

This is not a cynical theory. Berkoff is admiring, almost reverential, as he stacks up the images that combine into the big picture, a new religion. Pontius Pilate, famous for cleansing his hands of Jesus's blood by allowing the mob to demand a ritual execution, says: 'I wash my hands. People love gestures.'

The concept was horribly echoed by the US fascist leader, Greg Withrow, who founded the Aryan Youth Movement before pretending to denounce racism in order to infiltrate America's liberal establishment. Withrow staged his own crucifixion, by white supremacist thugs who were actually working on his orders. They drove nails through his hands in an empty parking lot.

In a lawsuit filed earlier this year, Withrow demanded: 'Could the greatest democracy on earth be fooled...with a board, two nails and a hammer? And if so, could this have been done 2,000 years ago in a more primitive society by a Jew?'

Steven Berkoff, who is Jewish, the son of an East End tailor, is an immensely charismatic man. He exudes strength, as hard as a plate of steel. His strength can be subtle, and a gentle vulnerability lies beneath the steel, visible even in the softness of his complexion.

He has a third eye which I can't stop staring at, a raised lump on his brow between his eyes, a tiny mound which is the focus of his whole face. In many ancient systems of wisdom, including yoga, human energy is concentrated at seven points of the body, like acupuncture pressure points. The third of these is precisely where the lump on Steven's forehead is. It's called the brow chakra, or the third eye, and it is the point through which all psychic impressions flow.

Modern science concurs: in brain scans done at the University of California, the part of the forebrain immediately behind the third eye glowed intensely when subjects meditated or experienced religious visions.

All good actors are psychic, but the degree of Berkoff's psychic energy is different. He is not merely interested in psi power – he knows it is his to wield, and he uses it instinctively.

When we met at Rabbi Pini Dunner's house a few months ago, we plunged immediately into a deep discussion of the untapped mind. He confessed to both bewilderment and excitement when he contemplated the unexplained, but not for an instant did he question it. Berkoff is not the sort of man who has to see a spoon bend before his curiosity is aroused.

I chickened out of playing Satan. The part was tempting, full of devilishly witty lines. The ruler of Hades is presented as a charming hate figure, in the tradition of another great dramatist who was also routinely accused of blasphemy – George Bernard Shaw.

Shaw's devil in *Man And Superman* had a superhuman number of lines to say. Berkoff's Beelzebub was less verbose, and I was intrigued by the challenge of taking and memorising someone else's word and making them my own.

Cornell John, who eventually took the part, is a tremendous actor, and I could not possibly have brought his brilliance or conviction to the role. But it is not that which makes me glad I refused. I identify myself with positive energy, and to have transformed myself into the essence of negativity night after night, repeating lines like mantras until they became indelibly etched on my mind, would have been spiritually dangerous.

I feared that my unconscious mind would rebel, as it did in the Seventies when I was asked – ordered, in fact – to take part in research and counter-espionage which ran against my moral instincts. Those troubling days culminated in a series of psychic phenomena over which I had no control. They were so frightening and strange that I might not be able to convince you of their reality if I described them for the next ten pages.

I have no fears for Cornell John, a powerful actor who is totally in command of his character. For myself, I had genuine anxieties. I never want to give the character of the devil a chance to take command of me.

PART 3

Personal Encounters

The people we meet do not always seem immediately significant. It is only when I reflect, perhaps many years later, on how a certain conversation became a turning point, that I realise every encounter throughout my life can be seen, in some way, to have been crucial. Even people whom I could not meet in person, because they had died before I was born – Sigmund Freud, Moshe Flinker, or, reaching back into Biblical history, the Prophet Ezekiel – prove in some way to have moulded my mind. These are my Personal Encounters.

About God

I ceased to believe in God in 1958. My mother had taken me to Cyprus, where my stepfather was trying to run a hotel during a civil war. I went to a Catholic school and already, at 12, before my Bar Mitzvah, I was feeling soul-lonely – the loneliness of a human being whose spirit has been exiled from its faith.

The newspapers loyal to each side fought a war of images, vying to outdo the enemy in reporting the atrocities. One sickening photograph has been imprinted on my mind ever since. Perhaps if I saw the original now – and I know I do not want to – it would be quite different from my memory. But I doubt it. This was an image which burned itself onto the retina like a magnesium flash.

There was a family, a Greek-Cypriot family. They had been murdered by Turkish-Cypriot terrorists and their bodies heaped into a bathtub. Two of the shocked, staring faces were clearly visible.

The caption said these people must have known their

killers. Their village was one of many ripped to tatters by the strife, neighbours and even in-laws thrown at each others' throats by the eruption of ancient race hatred.

To an Israeli boy, whose father had fought for a foothold on his homeland, it seemed tragically incomprehensible – families being slaughtered by former friends, because they shared an island idyll, one that had been common territory for hundreds of years.

Since 1958, of course, there have been so many more images of atrocity, via ever more vivid media. Black-and-white TV showing me the massacre in Biafra. Colour pictures of the aftermath of jungle battles in Vietnam, and video images of mass starvation in Africa.

Live footage from the nosecones of guided missiles. Web cameras giving minute-by-minute coverage of the sniper alleys in Bosnia. Rolling news coverage of the slaughter of a Palestinian boy in his father's arms, and the destruction of the Pentagon and the twin towers in the U.S.

But the picture in my mind will always be on crumpled, tattered newsprint, of a father and mother, a grandmother and their children, clustered in a mass of limbs that trailed over the side of a bath tub.

It was then, at 12 years old, that I first framed a basic charge against God: If you exist, how can you permit this? If you permit this, how can I feel anything but hatred for you? And if I hate you, and you permit such meaningless atrocities, wouldn't it be better for all the world if you did not exist?

And so God died. Many millions of others have killed him the same way. I happened to work it out for myself, but I'm certain someone would have planted the idea in my mind within a few years.

When my God was reborn, some time in my 30s, it was not as a white-bearded patriarch with the power to overturn human actions with a snap of his thunderbolt fingers. I do powerfully believe, and have never ceased to believe, that there are creatures of a higher intelligence and more sublime spirituality which possess that power of intervention. We sense them only as intangible flickers at the edge of reality – déjà vu, premonitions, flashes of telepathy.

Perhaps the creatures are God's angels. Maybe they are aliens. They are not God. Compared to the divine energy which suffuses all the universe, these creatures are as insignificant as we are.

For six months I have watched with growing puzzlement a debate among Bible archaeologists about Asherah, the wife of the Hebrew God. According to the Torah, Asherah must not exist – 'You shall have no other gods besides me,' decreed the white-bearded patriarch at the summit of Sinai.

But according to all the mythology of the Middle East, Asherah did exist, in almost infinite variations. In Abyssinia she was Astar, in Arabia Athtar, in Babylonia and Assyria Istar or Ishtar.

In Rome she was Astraea and in Persia Sitarah. In Greek the word is Astarte who among the Celts of Northern Europe was Ostare, Ostara, Ostern, Eostre, Eostur, Eastra and Eastur.

This word, of course, is also the Christian 'Easter'.

Evidence that Asherah was worshipped alongside Yahweh, a female deity who made his male godness whole, has been uncovered by Professor Ze'ev Herzog in Tel Aviv University's archaeology department. He has uncovered references at sites in Judah and further south, dating back only 2,800 years, which suggest Israel prayed to Asherah centuries after Solomon and David lived.

This idea has been refuted, with rising shrillness, by devout Jews on all sides. I count myself a true Jew, if not a devout one – and my pride in my people is strengthened by the concept of a female component in the divine. This makes us stronger, not weaker.

It seems that Jews knew, almost 3,000 years ago, what we supposed was a spiritual revelation so fresh that we call it 'New Age'. Our ancestors saw there was one God, and an all-powerful one. They understood this divine energy was present in events that were irreconcilable – feasts and famines, murders and miracles.

They expressed this in the most natural way, ascribing to God a feminine power as well as a masculine one. It was not a question of 'good' and 'evil', just as in a human marriage one partner is not saintly and the other wicked. Our forebears knew better than that.

It seems they might have known much better than us altogether. When we investigate the findings of scholars such as Professor Herzog, we should not be wondering, 'How does this compare to current theories?'

We should ask, more humbly, 'What have we forgotten which our ancestors knew?'

Rabbi Geller

Rabbi Geller has a pleasant ring to it. As a young man I hoped it would be Major Geller, and my mother perhaps dreamed it might be Dr Geller – later, prodded around by scientists, I fantasised of Professor Geller, even Nobel Laureate Geller. Even, if I got the chance to teach Prince Charles how to bend spoons, Lord Geller.

But Rabbi Geller is best. There is no other title which better suggests learning, spirituality, maturity and social importance. It requires many years of dedicated study, of course, and conventional religion was never my vocation, so until this week it never seemed likely that anyone would address me as 'Rabbi'.

But then I got this email, from Minister Charles Simpson. He informed me that he has the power to make me a legally ordained minister within 48 hours, giving me the authority to perform the rites and ceremonies of the church.

The Rev Simpson doesn't specify which church, but

there's nothing in the email to suggest that my Jewishness would be a problem. In fact, I'm invited to start my own church. How about Rabbi Geller of the Temple of the Curved Cutlery? Just kidding folks!

I'll be able to marry my brother, my sister or my best friend, promises the Reverend. Since I don't have a brother or sister, and my best friend says he wouldn't marry me even if I were single, I'm afraid the minister is promising too much – but perhaps he means that I would be able to conduct wedding ceremonies for family members. I'll be able to bury people too, and baptise babies. There's no mention of circumcisions or Bar Mitzvahs, but I'm sure my certificate will cover it.

One of the best offers – all included in the ordination fee of $29.95 plus $11 overseas shipping costs – is the power to forgive sins. All you have to do is ask me for absolution in all sincerity, demonstrating a willingness to change for the better, and I'll wipe your slate clean. I can do this, apparently, even if you're in a 'correctional facility'.

Rev Simpson is based in Oranjestad, chief port and capital of the Caribbean island of Aruba – a sunny outcrop of 75 square miles with an estimated population of 72,100. Aruba deliberately rejected independence from the Netherlands about five years ago, with virtually zero unemployment and an average income of $21,000.

How many of those jobs are in the church, I'm not certain, but clearly there's a good living to be had on Aruba, forgiving sins and visiting correctional facilities.

A search of the Web reveals other, even more exciting opportunities. Once I've been ordained, I can apply to the University of Esoterica to become a Doctor of Divinity or Theology. Divinity is the title to choose if I wish to style myself a seeker after the divine, a mystic, a counsellor or a teacher, a healer or an earth-based shaman.

As a Doctor of Divinity, I can sign myself as Rev Uri

Geller, D.Div. If I regard myself as more of a scholar, however, a lover of the written world and ancient scripture, a student of arcane lore, lost alphabets and forgotten languages, I should apply to be a Doctor of Theology and style myself Rev Uri Geller, ThD.

In fact, I see myself in both those roles, so I might opt to be a double doctor, a D.Div, ThD. The fee for each, payable to the Esoteric Theological Seminary is $600.

I ought to recoup my initial investment quite swiftly, since in the US I will be eligible for tax exemptions. Though I won't be able to charge for my services, I can invite donations and 'love offerings'. A wedding can command a love offering of $150, and a house blessing anything up to $1000.

The seminary's advisor notes: 'I know ministers who suggest hefty donations fees. As long as you're fine with it, and your customers are fine with it, it's FINE.' I'm not sure whether that means 'fine' as in a payment to a judge which might keep me out of a correctional facility.

To qualify for my doctorates, I shall have to submit a 2,000 word thesis of a spiritual nature. No problem – I'll send them one of my newspaper columns and I'm halfway there already.

All this is pleasantly ridiculous, but these dubious certificates wouldn't exist if there weren't people willing to pay for them, and many more people willing to believe in them. The dark side of such practices surfaces every time newspapers expose people performing hospital operations in the false guise of surgeons and people robbed in their homes by conmen claiming to be electrical engineers.

There's a lighter side too – one of the favourite scams in England's channel ports is for thieves to stop cars as they roll out of the ferries. The crooks announce themselves as plain-clothes customs officers and confiscate all the tobacco and alcohol on board.

I'll never be a minister. Not a real one, no matter how

many certificates I collect from cheesy websites. No one will ever call me Rabbi.

But I do have one title which means the world to me. Every hour of my life I strive to live up to this highest honour, to behave with the dignity and generosity and wisdom and kindness which it demands.

My children call me Aba, or Dad. To be worthy of that name is my greatest ambition.

Hypnotism

'Peace,' a politician told me recently, 'is not possible. A moment's peace, maybe – but lasting peace, no. Jews and Arabs are too different. We are different races, different cultures, these things will never be resolved. We are almost from different universes.'

This politician was the kind of man who frosts over when anyone is speaking except himself, and just standing with him made me feel poisoned. So I didn't try to attack his bigotry. I just walked away, glad that at the moment he holds no position of power.

He is wrong. Jews and Arabs are one humanity living in one world, alike in every respect except the most trivial and misleading details. I've seen the proof. And it was one of the most baffling experiences of my career.

I was on a downward bounce for the first time, in Israel early in 1972, when I'd been touring my show for something like 20 months. I had provoked a sensation with metal-bending and mind-reading, I had been endorsed by Prime Minister Golda Meir, I had had a lot of fun. But now my stage persona was well known. People thought I'd used up all my surprises. Later that year, the CIA came to inspect me, and launched me to worldwide fame by accident – but I'm talking about a time pre-CIA. To vary my performances, I had added hypnotism to the agenda.

One night I was at the Shavit auditorium in the lovely coastal town of Haifa. I went on after the film, demonstrated my powers, and launched into the hypnotics. I ordered everyone to clasp their hands. Of the 1,000 or so in the audience, about 200 would refuse – they were frightened of what might happen. They needn't have been – hypnotism cannot occur in an unwilling mind.

I began to count down, slowly and intently: 'Ten, nine, eight... your hands are gripping more firmly... seven, six, five... hey are tightly, tightly clasped... four, three, two... at the end of the countdown you will not be able to release your hands, no matter what... ONE!!!'

About 100 people would keep their hands bonded. I'd call them up on stage, all of them, and about 60 per cent would be faking. I could sense the fakers, the attention-seekers, at a dozen paces, and I'd send them curtly back to their seats. The remaining 30 or 40 would sit in a semi-circle on stage. I'd release their hands – and then the fun would begin.

They ate onions which I told them were apples, they talked like Mickey Mouse and Donald Duck, they danced like Nureyev and chuffed round the stage like the Orient Express. The showstopper was a flight around the world, 'We are nearing the equator... you're very warm... you're getting hot... too hot... you must take off your shirt, it's so hot... phew, and your trousers... it's so hot... and – NO!! Not the underpants, we're near the Arctic Circle now and you're cold suddenly... quick, on with the clothes!'

After that, I would regress them. Again I counted down from ten, and by the count of five they were five years old, three at the count of three, two, then one...If I went all the way to zero, I had a stage of helpless, bawling, burping adults.

Once I went beyond zero. Into the minus numbers.

One of the people on stage was a man of 21 or so, with a long jaw and coal-black eyes. He was an excellent subject – the depth of his hypnotic trance shone in his gaze. He had given himself up fearlessly to the experience, and when I had regressed him to the womb and then back still further – he went.

He was a Moroccan, he told me later, but when I asked him who he was, he replied in Polish: 'My name is Leopold.'

I do not speak Polish, but I knew enough Poles, Russians and Czechs to be able to tell the languages apart. My surprise was that this young man, much swarthier than most Ashkenazi, knew it.

'I need an interpreter,' I yelled out, and a middle-aged man came hurrying onto the stage. By the time he had clambered up he was wheezing, and his breaths sounded like hinges creaking when I handed him my microphone.

For the next 15 minutes, I let my subject talk. He spoke in a measured and constant voice, so that the interpreter had to work hard to keep up without missing a word. The story they told had no beginning, no middle but a very definite end. The subject remembered horses, and how every week he had to travel 40 miles along dirt roads, starting at daybreak from his village and ending after dark in Warsaw. He was taking produce to market – little of it, and that which he took fetched a poor price. But this, he said, was what a country man must expect and, after all, he did not need to pay city prices to live, so the few zlotys his vegetables and his skins would fetch could last his family comfortably through the week.

He described how he would return home on a Thursday night, and Friday's preparations for the Sabbath. He told us what they ate, and how they prayed, and for every person in that movie theatre it was a moving testimony. Then he talked of his death – 'great coughing, and a pain behind my ribs that lasted many days and nights, so that I was glad when it ceased, so glad I did not care what would become of me'. That was the last thing he said in Polish, and I was suddenly anxious to bring my subject out of his trance. Although it had seemed fun to talk somebody backwards beyond their own birth, it felt dangerous to let him talk forwards through his own death – and beyond.

But as I leant over to break the spell, the translator was struck by a notion and asked, 'What was the king's name?'

'Stanislaw,' he answered.

We looked up the monarchs of Poland later, and saw Stanislaw II ruled around the time of the French Revolution. The translator claimed this made sense, as the man's Polish was old-fashioned and rustic.

But what astonished me even more than this detailed memory of a past life – and I can think of nothing that explains all the details, except to admit that we live again and again – was the subject's story when he awoke. He was not an Israeli. He was not even a Jew. He was a Moroccan, in Israel on an American passport to visit friends.

He was an Arab, named Mohammed. A Moslem.

An Arab Moslem who had been, without any doubt, a Polish Jew.

An eye for an eye

When I was a few months old, a British sniper's bullet shattered the window of my parents' apartment in Tel Aviv, showering my crib with glass. My memory of the cold shards on my face, of my mother's screams and my own, may be images reconstructed from subconscious echoes – but I remember clearly how my father showed me, years later, the hole in the wall where the bullet struck.

I have always felt that brush with death made me forever an Israeli. Though I was sent to school in Cyprus, and made famous in America, and feted in Mexico, and though I found peace in Japan and raised my family in England, I am an Israeli. Like Israel, I was birthed in war.

In 1991, when Saddam Hussein fired salvoes of Soviet-made surface-to-air Scud missiles at Jerusalem and Tel Aviv, I feared Israel would retaliate, and our State, and probably the whole world, would find its death in war.

It rapidly became plain that Saddam was not arming the

Scuds with chemical or biological weaponry – much later we learned that the US-made Patriot missiles, credited with intercepting all but two Scuds, in fact missed their mark every time. A US Army spokesman said President George Bush had not been lying, because 'intercept does not mean destroyed; it means a Patriot and a Scud passed in the sky'.

I do not think Israel's courage in the Gulf War has been fully acknowledged. We are a nation inured to war – but when Saddam bombed our cities to provoke us, we defied him.

Now we have to summon the same kind of bravery to defuse a different kind of crisis. Following the terrorist attack on the US and the subsequent reprisals on Afghanistan, everything has changed. Our world and the order in which we lived, and which the West had taken for granted, has been shaken to its very core.

We all know that allied jets had been bombing Iraq for years. Until now the West did not seem to care. Many believed it to be a just and necessary action taken to punish Iraq for its unjust and unwarranted aggression. In addition, subsesequent sanctions have been slowly squeezing the life out of the country. There is no sign they will be lifted.

We bombed Iraq because its mad despotic leader once threatened us with a conflict too awful to contemplate. In Afghanistan we have been faced with a fugitive for an enemy and a terrorist threat that cannot be underestimated.

But nor must we underestimate the anger that festers in extremists in the Middle East, people driven to insanities in the name of religion and revenge. When an American AGM-130 missile ploughed into a Basra housing complex in Iraq, 17 people died and 100 were wounded. These are United Nations figures. Ten of the dead were children. Six more were women.

The figures are negligible compared to the human cost of sanctions. The UN children's fund (Unicef) estimated that between 5,000 and 6,000 Iraqi children die of disease and starvation every month. The mortality rate for under-fives has more than tripled since sanctions were imposed, and a quarter of infants are malnourished.

Nasra al Sa'adoun, the Sorbonne-educated granddaughter of an Iraqi Prime Minister, told Western journalists in Baghdad, 'We have no electricity, no clean water, no trains, no safe cars, and you are bombing us every day. I tell you, we would rather have a real war than this slow death. This is genocide.'

Genocide is not too strong a word. The ten-year total for child deaths caused by sanctions is put at 500,000. Unicef, the World Health Organisation (WHO) and ex-officials of the UN such as Denis Halliday, who was Humanitarian Co-ordinator for Iraq, all testify to these estimates.

Health-care has dwindled to nothing. The UN reported, 'Public health services are near total collapse – basic medicines, life-saving drugs and essential medical supplies are lacking throughout the country.'

Useless components for vital equipment gather dust in Iraq's warehouses, because sanctions make it impossible to import even life-saving products in practical ways. Syringe plungers arrive one year – medics are still waiting for the needles 12 months on. The UN, struggling to render such a humanitarian blunder in bureaucratic jargon, says this is a problem of 'uncomplementarity'.

Most horrific of all is the tenfold increase in cancers. Within ten years 44 per cent of Iraqis will develop cancer, according to John Hopkins University and Baghdad's Profesor Mikdem M Saleh. Radiation levels in Basra are 84 times above WHO safety limits, and the city hospital sees grotesquely deformed foetuses and babies every day.

This horror has been caused by the radioactive DU (depleted uranium) which is used to coat Allied warheads.

DU is increasingly used instead of titanium as a low-cost, armour-piercing outer shell on missiles. Some estimates suggest 900 tonnes of radioactive waste, which will cease to be hazardous only after 4.5 billion years, litters Iraq.

There can be no justification for murder and mass slaughter on the scale that we have seen in the United States. But let us remind ourselves of where the seeds of hatred are sown. If we do not address these issues then we run the risk of becoming locked in a deadly game of anger and retribution. Any eye for an eye leaves everyone blind.

Memories of Yom Kippur

Memory is extraordinary. Trivial thoughts can wander through our minds, and return forty years later laden with meaning. I was reading the Torah on Rosh Hashanah, [the Jewish New Year] a year ago, and a childhood daydream came back to me that was born of boredom then. Now it fills my head with wonder.

The trigger was a long catalogue of ritual sacrifices in the Book of Numbers. For verse after verse, Moses is told what animals shall be slain, and which shall be offered as meals, and how they must be cooked. The same phrases are echoed and re-echoed, in an almost endless combination.

To an adult, who has spent years studying the hypnotic force of words, this is one of the most fascinating passages of the Bible. To a child, it was interminable. When I began to read it aloud in my garden, I remembered a scratchy, droning, male voice reciting the same verses. I believe the rabbi was an old man, who addressed my school occasionally on days of great significance. You could stare straight into his face, because he never looked up at us, and I found this interesting because most grown-ups would let me gaze at them for only so long before flashing a stare back at me.

The verses meant little then. They were just a holy shopping list. And I remember thinking, 'How did Moses remember them? This list is so long, and its changes are so minute and so precise.'

The rabbi was reading, 'On the tenth day of the same seventh month you shall observe a sacred occasion when you shall practice self-denial. You shall do no work. You shall present to the Lord a burnt offering of pleasing odour: one bull of the herd, one ram, seven yearling lambs; see that they are without blemish. The meal offering with them – of choice flour with oil mixed in – shall be: three tenths of a measure for a bull, two tenths for the one ram, one-tenth for each of the seven lambs. And there shall be one goat for a sin offering...'

And so the old rabbi talked on – one day thirteen bulls, another fourteen yearling lambs, another two rams – until he concluded, 'So Moses spoke to the Israelites just as the Lord had commanded Moses.'

Impious thoughts come easily to children, and the one buzzing in my brain was: 'How could Moses be certain? Even if he was taking notes, was he absolutely sure he'd got every detail right? Because he couldn't go back to God and ask, 'Sixth day, seventh month, is that fourteen bulls or eight?'

These are not the sort of daydreams a child should reveal to the rabbi, unless he wants his ears boxed.

But in my garden last year, I was struck again by the question. Even admitting that Moses must have been right in every detail, how could all the priests through all the centuries keep the list perfect and uncorrupted?

The answer, like the answers to many difficult questions,

came at Yom Kippur. At the afternoon service at a London synagogue, the rabbi began the short version of the Vidui [Confession] which starts, 'Ashamnu, bagadnu, gazalnu...' which translated means, we sinned, we betrayed, we robbed...'

For the first time I was struck by the alphabetic sequence of the words. The pattern was beautifully woven, from alef-bet-gimel, [the first three letters of the Hebrew alphabet] without ever becoming forced or contorted. When I looked at the long version, I was dazzled – that too followed the alphabet, in a form which crossword solvers call 'acrostic'.

These words were written thousands of years before crossword compilers began their word games. Why would God play with words? For fun? That was a science fiction thought – the Tanakh as a divine doodle, drawn up over cups of celestial coffee.

There had to be a serious reason for the wordplay. And, since I've spent much of my life teaching people to super-charge their brains, the reason was clear – memory power.

We remember patterns. A jumble of words is easily memorised if arranged in any kind of order. The memory wizards who stand on stage and reel off packs of shuffled cards in sequence have learned to impose patterns on any kind of chaos. This knowledge is widely taught today, though few schools help pupils to use it – I've never understood why not. But in rabbi school, millennia ago, these same secrets were taught.

The recurring phrases are part of the pattern – 'See that they are without blemish,' 'Of choice flour with oil mixed in,' 'One goat for a sin offering'. To the pious listener or the bored schoolboy, the rabbi's memory appears miraculous. When the technique is revealed, the miracle is understood – and no less marvellous.

The professors of religious history generally agree that Judaism's indestructibility dates from the invention of writing. The first words were recorded in the Middle East, and while the Egyptians were still combining pictures to capture their thoughts, the Israelites had a far more powerful tool – the alphabet.

Most people would never learn to read, of course, and the most sacred of texts were vulnerable to destruction. I believe writing was essential, but not alone, in preserving our religion.

Memory was the key. The ability to recall immense swathes of information – laws, histories, rituals, marvels. Word for word, without change. Memory meant survival.

Schroeder and the science of God

The pollster George Gallup once said, 'I could prove God statistically. Take the human body alone – the chance that all the functions of the individual would just happen is a statistical monstrosity.'

Polls aren't always right, but they are usually accurate about landslides. And the statistical evidence that we were created, not evolved by chance, is more than a landslide – it's an avalanche on Everest.

Nobel prize-winning physicist Steven Weinberg puts it like this: 'Life as we know it would be impossible if any one of several physical quantities had slightly different values…One constant does seem to require incredible fine tuning.' That constant concerns the energy emitted during the Big Bang – make it bigger, or smaller, by one trillion trillion trillion trillion trillion trillion trillion trillion trillion trillionth and life could never have existed.

The Fermilab astrophysicist Michael Turner adds, 'The

155

precision is as if one could throw a dart across the entire universe and hit a bullseye one millimetre in diameter on the other side.'

All our natural instincts, all our religious beliefs, all our culture and our myths and now even our statisticians, point to the existence of God the creator. But science points in the other direction, towards evolution and random mutation and blind chance. And science has an extraordinary record of being right. We see the miraculous rightness of science in the atom bomb and the television and the space shuttle and the mobile phone, all of them impossible fantasies a century ago.

Dr Gerald Schroeder, a former professor of nuclear physics at the Massachusetts Institute of Technology and a member of the US Atomic Energy Commission, knows science has the power to win any existential argument. I met him in Jerusalem and then, by synchronicity (or a mild quirk of statistics), in London a few days later.

'You can't argue with atomic physics,' he told me. 'I personally have witnessed the detonation of six nuclear weapons and my advice is, pray for peace. Pray for peace.

'Mere fractions of a gram of matter were converted to energy during those tests, in Nevada, and the mountain I stood on was turned to a quivering, Jello-like substance.'

Schroeder talks the way he moves, in quick jerks, with an energy that is unnerving in his gaunt body. He wears a faded, embroidered kippah, clamped to his thin hair with broad silver clips, and pokes fun at his piety, 'When I was a kid, the synagogue I just about never went to was Orthodox.'

Not much about organised religion is sacred to Schroeder. What he believes in is the Bible, and he is battling to prove that the Bible was right all along. From Moses to Einstein is, he claims, a very short step.

The six days of creation, for instance, become a workable timeframe when Einstein's General Theory of Relativity is invoked. In his book *The Science of God* Schroeder explains that time on a planet such as Earth appears to pass with lightning rapidity to observers at points in space where gravity is immensely powerful – in a black hole, for instance.

To a God of universal vastness, 5 million years on Earth would be the blink of an eye. Schroeder sets out the days of creation in a fascinating cross-table of creation and astrophysics, beginning on Day One, 15.75 billion years ago, when 'God separated the light from the darkness' – after the Big Bang, says Schroeder, light literally broke free as electrons bonded to atomic nuclei.

Day Two, between 7.75bn and 3.75bn years ago, 'God called the expanse sky' – the disc of the Milky Way, including the sun, was formed.

Day Three, between 3.75bn and 1.75bn years ago, 'God called the dry land Earth and the gathering of waters He called Seas'– the appearance of liquid water was immediately followed by the arrival of bacteria and photosynthetic algae.

Day Four, between 1.75bn and 0.75bn years ago, 'God made the two great lights ... to dominate the day and the night' – Earth's increasingly oxygen-rich atmosphere became transparent.

Day Five, between 0.75bn and 0.25bn years ago, 'God created ... all the living creatures of every kind that creep, which the waters brought forth in swarms' – sealife developed the blueprints of all future animals, before colonisation of the land began.

Day Six, between 250 million and 6,000 years ago, 'God created man in his image' – following the extinction of the dinosaurs, hominids and then humans appeared.

Gerald Schroeder is not a Creationist of the US Bible Belt kind. He is not demanding our schools cease to teach Darwin. He is stating that the Bible, properly interpreted, is first-rate science.

And he is fulfilling the great physicist Max Planck's manifesto, 'There can never be any real opposition between religion and science; for the one is the complement of the other. Every serious and reflective person realises...that the religious element in his nature must be recognised and cultivated if all the powers of the human soul are to act together in perfect balance and harmony. And indeed it was not by accident that the greatest thinkers of all ages were deeply religious souls...Science enhances the moral values of life...because every advance in knowledge brings us face to face with the mystery of our own being.'

We can only pray that this science, created by religious souls will not destroy us.

Ruth and the cult

Ruth has come home. After two years and two months in a San Francisco commune, refusing even to speak to her family until recent weeks, she has now moved back in with her mother and father in Boston.

I have known her since she was a child – her father is a scientist who worked with me at Livermore in the Seventies. She used to insist I must only speak Hebrew to her, to help her studies – she dreamt of becoming a rabbi. She was not even ten years old then. Now she is a Christian, recruited by a cult which targets Jews for conversion, and I should be rejoicing at her escape. I cannot – the whole episode has made me profoundly anxious, for Ruth and for thousands of young Jews.

Ruth says she was brainwashed. She says she's finished with this bunch, the 'Jesus Jews', and with all cults, forever. But she is going to remain a Christian. She is back with her parents, but not back at synagogue, and I don't think her war is over.

The Jesus Jews are more stalkers than evangelists. They saw a lonely, confused girl, thousands of miles from home, and they set out to snare her. Everything she had believed and everyone she had loved had to be discarded. It was a sick power game, one that is being played out all over California and the southern states.

The first I heard of it was a late-night phone-call from Ruth's father, Richard. He'd just talked with his daughter, who had been out in San Fransisco for three months with a software firm, and he was worried about her new friends. They were all Ruth could talk about – a couple of girls, Debbie and Anat, and an older man who called himself Abram. All Jewish, all evangelical Christians.

They had met outside the synagogue, where Ruth was accosted by the girls who wanted her to meet 'a special friend'. The special friend turned out to be 'Jesus'. Abram claimed Jesus came to him as he lay unconscious at the wheel of his car after an accident, and ordered him to devote his life to coverting his fellow Jews to Christianity.

'We are God's chosen people, Jesus said that to me,' Abram told Ruth. 'That's why he's so grieved that Jews won't accept his son as the Messiah, because he'll be forced to consign them to the flames of hell for eternity. That upsets him. You don't want to make God sad, do you, Ruth? Turn to Jesus and you'll make him so happy, he'll weep tears of joy. Make God happy. Be a Jesus Jew.'

Ruth's father could not believe his educated, intelligent, knowing daughter could have heard one word of that spiel without laughing in contempt. But he had not counted on her loneliness. Cut off from her family and her friends, unhappy at work and perhaps nursing an unconscious guilt that she had not fulfilled her childhood promise to be a rabbi, Ruth was willing to abandon everything in her life to search of love and happiness.

Debbie and Anat offered friendship. Abram offered Jesus's love and eternal salvation. She could still be a Jew, they said, she could still say Jewish prayers and read a Jewish Bible – though they forbade her to attend synagogue, and she was told to focus on photocopied extracts from the New Testament, instead of being allowed to open a whole Bible.

The calls home soon stopped. Ruth wouldn't hear any criticism of the cult, and she refused to reveal anything about them – not even where they lived, though she now lived with them. She kept working, but all her earnings went to the Jesus Jews, to be shared between them, 'Jesus loves us all equally,' said Abram, 'so it would be bad if any of us had more than the others.'

And then the letter came, when Ruth told her mother and father they were under the control of Satan, and if she was to protect her soul she must never see them again. Richard flew to San Fransisco and spent a week tracking his daughter – she had warned her employers to tell him nothing, but at last he found her address through a Jesus Jews pamphlet. She refused to see him. He says now that she was mentally ill, and will not blame her for what happened

But if it is an illness, it is one deliberately inflicted by the Jesus Jews. The Task Force on Missionaries and Cults states: 'Approximately 3,000 cults exist in the United States today. There are over 200 missionary groups in the United States (with a combined budget of over $100 million) specifically targeting Jewish people for conversion. More than 100,000 American Jews have been converted by missionary groups in the past 20 years, and a disproportionate number of Jews have joined cults.'

Ruth came home, after more than two years. Her rescue began with a call to her father on his birthday – she pretended she had done it without thinking, on the spur of the moment, but it took a lot of courage. She missed her family so badly that the brainwashing about Richard being a puppet of Satan gradually stood out in her mind as an impossible lie. If the Jesus Jews lied to her about that, she asked herself, what else had been lies?

Everything. It was all lies. That's what she says now. Richard just prays that when she says it, she means it.

Moshe's diary

I have a guiding law, when I am in any city, that I will follow my impulses without questioning them too much. If I see a cab and want to hail it, I'll hail it – when the window slides down I'll decide where to go. If I want to walk up a sidestreet, or turn back on myself, I do. We all get these sudden urges – I believe they are messages from our subconscious minds. They lead us where we need to go. By obeying an impulse, I discovered Moshe Flinker's diary.

I had been meeting a journalist friend at the *Guardian*, and left the building intending to turn right down London's Farringdon Road, towards the Thames – but my subconscious said 'Turn left!' At a set of lights I crossed, strolling up a wide boulevard of pavement cafés called Exmouth Market, past a church and betting shops. These were not what put my psychic sense on alert.

Outside a bookshop eight or ten big boxes were overspilling with old paperbacks and discarded library copies. It was a hot day and the covers were curling in the sunshine. This was stock the shopkeeper could hardly be bothered to sell. A notice was taped on the window: 'All Books Outside, £1'.

Lying face-up on the nearest box, where I could not fail to miss it, was 'Young Moshe's Diary'. A black-and-white ID photo of a boy's unsmiling face stared up. Below the irises of his eyes a crescent of white beneath the iris betrayed tiredness and ill-nourishment. A subtitle read: 'The spiritual torment of a Jewish boy in Nazi Europe'.

Moshe Flinker died aged 17 in Auschwitz. For nearly two years he and his family lived under false papers in Brussels, keeping a low profile, disguising their Jewishness, bribing officials. Back in Amsterdam, the city the Flinkers fled in the summer of 1942, Otto Frank and his family were taking refuge in a secret annexe above a warehouse on Prinzengracht.

Anne Frank's diary is probably the best-known book of the twentieth century, filled with unflinching insight into human weaknesses and pettiness. She knew her own talent as a writer, and was editing her entries for eventual publication when the family were betrayed.

Moshe Flinker's diary is all but forgotten. Written in classical Hebrew, it is almost empty of detail about his parents and his siblings.

But Moshe too had an eye for publication, and his thoughts are filled with a poet's delight in what it means to be Jewish, and how all Jews must work together to create an Israel worthy of God.

Moshe was not only a deeply spiritual thinker with an extraordinary faith. He was also a fledgling statesman. Anyone reading his diary cannot doubt that, if this young man had survived the war, he would have fulfilled his ambition, to be 'a Jewish statesman in the Land of Israel'.

He had an acute political instinct, guessing from news

reports the Allies' strategic aims and Russia's long-term plans. By August 1943 he had seen that Stalin would annex Europe and that Roosevelt was already preparing for the post-war carve-up. He guessed too that Germany could not be bombed into surrender.

Sitting in his room throughout every day, because he had no place at any school and to be seen on the streets was inviting arrest, Moshe studied. He was teaching himself Arabic, to make himself a diplomat for the new Jewish nation. What political disasters a mind like Moshe's could have averted for Israel in the Fifties and Sixties.

His view of human nature was simple, noble and sometimes breathtakingly naive. He sometimes despised himself for surviving when friends were seized: 'I feel that I have not been saved for the future of my people; on the contrary, I see myself as if I were a traitor, who fled from his people at the time of their anguish.'

He even contemplated volunteering for the camps: 'I often have a great yearning for my brothers who are in Poland and elsewhere...I realise that it is actually possible to reach them. The Germans want many workers everywhere...so that I should go to the Germans and say that I wish to go and work and then they would doubtlessly take me.'

And they did take him, and all his family, on 7 April 1944, Passover eve. An informer led the Gestapo to the apartment, where the matzot [unleavened bread] was ready and meat lay after its ritual salting in the kitchen. Though his parents died in Auschwitz too, the boy's five sisters and his brother survived, and several made their home in Israel.

An inquiry at Amazon, the internet bookshop, reveals the English translation of 'Hana'ar Moshe – Yomano shel Moshe Flinker' is out of print, though extracts are published in 'We Are Witnesses: Five diaries of children who died in the Holocaust'.

The ordeal of hundreds of thousands of Jews in hiding will always be remembered, because of Anne Frank's razor-edged writing. Moshe's diary should be rediscovered and treasured for a different reason – it is a huge-hearted clarion call to all of mankind.

Elvis and Lotte

The first sign that something was wrong came as I picked the box up. Glass tinkled. I called my wife over and we started to strip back the packing tape. 'Someone has opened this already,' she said.

Daggers of fine glass lay on the bubble wrap inside. 'Don't touch it,' warned Hanna. She hurried away and returned with thick gardening gloves and a newspaper.

We carefully removed the glass and lifted the layers of plastic. At the bottom of the box lay the rare Elvis Presley recording I had purchased on an internet auction site for $1,000. It had been bent double. Because the acetate had been mounted on metal before being framed, it had not snapped. But it was beyond repair.

I phoned the vendor in the United States – he swore it had left him in good condition. I phoned the police and the parcels office – they were sympathetic, but could not help, since the package had come from abroad.

All of them joked politely that I was Uri Geller, and the record was bent, and well, you know...

Strange things do happen around me. The way I found this disc online was one: on the day I launched my latest novel, *Nobody's Child*, a friend called to say she'd seen a good investment opportunity on the Web. An unreleased Elvis song, which until now had existed only in rumour, recorded in his truck-driver days, was up for auction. The bidding was quiet... and I wouldn't believe what the track was called, 'Nobody's Child.'

Compared to that coincidence, the idea that the acetate spontaneously self-destructed seems almost probable.

But I have many valuable metal artworks, including a Dali sculpture, and though I admit I sometimes care about them more than I should, I cannot remember one instance when my metal-bending energy caused damage.

One explanation was suggested by a journalist friend with a suspicious mind. 'Imagine a guy needs a little money,' he said. 'He advertises on an auction website that he has a rare, unreleased pop recording by a dead superstar, unlisted in the discographies – Buddy Holly before he was famous, say, or maybe Elvis...

'Actually what he has is an old Sixties acetate his Dad cut in a 10 cent recording booth. He copies a label from a book on his PC, doctors the wording, prints it out and gums it down. Then he mounts the disc, photographs it in a frame and waits for the bids.

'After the sale, he carefully packages it up. Then he breaks open the box, smashes the frame and bends the disc double. He reseals the box, scrappily, and mails it off.

'He assumes the purchaser will have taken out insurance on his expensive toy, so no one is really getting ripped off.

'The only danger is that an insurance investigator will take the disc to a data recovery expert who might extract a few seconds of sound from the mangled acetate. But that could cost hundreds of dollars, so he's probably safe.

'In the worst case scenario, he is accused of the crime: but he looks innocent and explains that the disc was in the frame when he bought it, he never played it, he sold in good faith, etc.'

Of course, I don't imagine that happened. I am more and more convinced that Elvis did it.

But so many things are not what they seem. Take Lotte Krautheimer, whose picture was painted 89 years ago.

Lotte was two years old, a beautiful girl with golden curls living with her parents in Furth, Germany. She caught the eye of Ludwig von Zumbusch, a popular painter, who used her as his model for a sentimental picture called Blondchen.

More than two decades later, Blondchen was Hitler's darling. Not the girl herself – she had moved to Sweden with her mother, who detested Nazism. It was the painting the Fuhrer adored, and the blue-eyed toddler was the image of the Aryan child who would inherit the Third Reich from his glorious regiments.

Hitler ordered copies of the painting to be hung in public places throughout Germany. It became particularly popular as a postcard.

Lotte did not discover she was a Nazi pin-up until long after the war. A doctor named Bauer visiting her home was shocked to see the propaganda image above her bed. 'But that's me!' Lotte protested.

Now 91, Lotte still remembers how her mother, Martha, combed her blonde curls before she sat for von Zumsbusch. There was another little girl, Lotte's older sister, but she and her husband were rounded up in Paris in 1942. They died in Auschwitz.

Lotte and her parents were Jewish. Hitler, of course, could not have known that. Things are so often not what they seem.

Popes and saints

Edgardo Mortara was two years old when he contracted a fever. His parents feared he would die as he lay in his cot, and begged their rabbi and friends in Bologna's small Jewish community to pray for the boy's recovery.

The Mortara's servant girl also wanted to intercede with God for the child. But she was a Catholic, devout and simple-minded, and she truly believed that the little boy's soul would be cast down into the Christian hell if he died unbaptised.

Under the pretence of mopping his burning face, she sprinkled water over his brow to baptise him.

The boy survived, and the maid told her priest what she had done. Four years later, pressed by hardline advisers who claimed canon law obliged the Church to care for every baptised child, Pope Pius IX ordered police to seize Edgardo from his parents, to drag him from his six brothers and sisters.

Despite the pleas of his parents, which roused international condemnation of the Vatican, Edgardo never saw his family again. He was more or less adopted by Pius as a son, and became a priest. After his death in 1940, his diaries revealed a tormented and guilt-ridden mind. Edgardo was far from being the only Jewish boy baptised into the Catholic faith in the teeth of his family's pleadings and anguish.

During his reign, between 1846 and 1878, Pius banned Jews in the papal states from receiving secondary and higher education, limited their rights to hold property or take employment, and ruled their evidence was inadmissable in court.

He laid the ground for the rise of genocidal anti-Semitism in Italy and across Europe. Yet Pius IX was beatified – the first stage of his elevation to sainthood.

It is hard to understand how a Pope who prayed at the Wailing Wall in Jerusalem this year could regard such a man as saintly. It is hard to imagine how this promotion could have been conceived as anything except a deliberate insult to Judaism. Even the Catholic writer Margaret Hebblethwaite said, 'It is gratuitously offensive to Jews. It is silly. But the Vatican is not very sensitive to criticism.'

Pope John Paul II is no anti-Semite. His ambition, in the words of the former *Catholic Herald* editor Cristina Odone, 'is to place his Church at the heart of a new religious alliance that would bring together Jews, Muslims and Christians in a great armada of God's troops on earth'.

Growing up in Wadowice, southern Poland, the man who was then still Karol Wojtyla lived in a house owned by a Jewish family. He played football for the town's Jewish team and his closest friend, then and now, is 80-year-old Jerzy Kluger.

Karol's first, and perhaps only, love affair was with a Jewish girl, Ginka Beer, who was said to have 'stupendous dark eyes and jet black hair'. She was also 'slender' and 'a superb actress', and Karol developed a sudden and irresistible interest in the theatre which compelled him to attend all Ginka's rehearsals.

Decades later she visited him, among a group of his old friends, at the Vatican. When the Pope remembered Ginka's mother fondly, he was shocked to learn she had been killed at Auschwitz.

Of 1500 Jews in Wadowice, only 80 survived the Holocaust.

'We have a paradox here,' remarked Elan Steinberg, of the World Jewish Congress. Paradox is an understatement. Here is the first Pope to visit a synagogue, the Pope who decreed anti-Semitism was sinful, now declaring that a child-snatcher and a Jew-hater is ripe to be called a saint.

Few would be surprised now if Pius XII, who ignored the Nazi slaughter of Jews and even promoted it, became a candidate for beatification.

I believe this can only be understood by regarding the roster of saints with a worldly Jewish eye. Most Christians, Catholic or not, believe a saint must certainly have been a very good, kind and spiritual person. The first saint to spring to anyone's mind would be Francis of Assisi, a kind of Gandhi of the Middle Ages, who talked with animals and healed with a touch of his hands.

I believe people like him have existed in our history – but very few of them. Most have earned the distrust or outright anger of the Church, the upper classes and their governments – nothing is more dangerous to the establishment than a man or woman of true principles.

One of this rare and inspirational figures was Padre Pio of Pietrelcina, a priest whose hands and feet wept blood from stigmata – mysterious wounds with no physical cause, following the pattern of Jesus's crucifixion scars. He had no prospect of a sainthood, for he defied the Vatican throughout most of his career.

St Francis was also a stigmatic. So too is a teenage Catholic girl, Audrey Santo, who lives near Boston, Massachusetts. She has been in a coma since 1987, but many thousands say she, like Padre Pio, has answered their prayers for healing.

These people are rare and miraculous. They deserve the veneration and love of all humanity. Karol Wojtyla too is a figure of inspiration to many, who is said to possess a marvellous gift of healing.

But when the Pope acts to beatify anti-Semites and kidnappers, we know 'sainthood' can sometimes have nothing to do with saintliness. The title 'Saint' can often be used as a politician's bauble, as meaningful as a life peerage or a civil servant's long-service medal.

No one, of any religion, should look to political 'saints' for inspiration and guidance. Turn instead to the rarest and best of humanity – the truly good.

Edward Said and Freud

The request from a BBC television researcher was one I have heard more and more in recent years: could I shed any light on rumours of a psychic experiment involving Albert Einstein and Sigmund Freud in Vienna, before the First World War?

I make no secret of my slender connections to the two gurus of twentieth century science. I was tested by the American theoretical physicist David Bohm, who had been a member of the Manhattan Project which developed the atom bomb and who was a personal friend of Einstein. I am prouder still of my relation to Freud through my mother's lineage.

But the only evidence I know of a meeting between these extraordinary pioneers is an anecdote in the biography of Wolf Messing, the brilliant Russian psychic who created a fabulous mythology around his career.

Messing claimed that in November 1913 he attended a gathering in Freud's Viennese apartment at Berggasse 19. The psychoanalyst proposed a telepathy experiment: he would issue a mental command to Messing.

'I will never forget it,' said the psychic. 'Go to the dressing table, pick up the tweezers, walk over to Einstein and pull out three hairs from his luxuriant moustache...I explained apologetically what his friend wanted me to do. Einstein smiled and submissively presented his cheek to me.'

Mind-bending though this image is, the *Psychoanalytical Review* has published an even stranger story. Professor Stanley Schneider and Dr Joseph Berke have claimed in the prestigious New York quarterly published by the National Psychological Association for Psychoanalysis that the fifth Lubavitcher rebbe, Dov-Ber Schneerson, met Freud several times around 1903.

According to notes made by the sixth rebbe – Schneerson's son – the Orthodox Jew and the atheist Jew spoke deeply about connecting spirit and consciousness.

'Are not the head and the heart two completely separated continents?' asked Freud. 'Does not a great sea divide them?'

The rebbe replied, 'The task is to build a bridge that will span these two continents, or at least connect them with telephone lines and electric wires so that the light of the mind should reach the heart as well.'

Freud's humility and his spiritual curiosity are badly needed today by the Viennese society which bears his name. The group, based at Berggasse 19, has cancelled a lecture by the Palestinian intellectual Edward Said, after a photograph was published of him preparing to hurl a stone at an Israeli guardhouse on the Lebanese border.

The picture is a shocking one. This eminent professor of English and comparative literature at Columbia University, educated at Princeton and Harvard, who is also a professional music critic and the author of ten books, has his arm drawn back. A snarl distorts his face.

His self-justification gave us one of the great excuses of the Intifada – he claimed to be having a stone-throwing contest with his son. Apparently the Palestinian uprising is just a game of marbles which got out of control. Either that, or Professor Said has lost his marbles altogether.

He also said the guardhouse was unoccupied and half-a-mile distant, the stone was a mere pebble and his action was a symbolic expression of joy at the withdrawal of Israeli forces from Lebanon.

The Freud Society's president, Johann August Schulein, wasn't buying the excuses. He wrote to Said, calling off the lecture in view of 'the political development in the Middle East and the consequences expected'.

Said called the cancellation outrageous. 'Freud was hounded out of Vienna because he was a Jew. Now I am hounded out because I am a Palestinian.'

The comparison is tasteless – Freud fled to Hampstead in London at the end of his life after Nazi troops marched into his house in 1938.

But the Society cannot claim to be ignorant of Said's views. He is one of the most forceful and eloquent advocates of the Palestinian grievances, frequently comparing the Arab pleas for an independent state to the African National Congress's fight against apartheid in South Africa.

He is clear-sighted about the depth of the problem. Writing in *Al-Ahram*, the Cairo-based weekly, Said admitted the Middle East conflict was more complex than the South African one, 'One people paid and the other is still paying a very heavy price in dispossession.'

He is committed to one side – as I am to the other – but he is honest enough to recognise that, to outside observers, the situation is impossible because both cultures have suffered so much.

Said also knows that without a leader of the charismatic

stature of Nelson Mandela, the Palestinians are doomed to the indifference of the West. He describes how he heard Mandela plead 'for all of us to assert our common humanity', and he knows that it is not a cry heard in Gaza or on the West Bank.

Without such a figure to inspire the peace-makers, peace may not be possible.

Instead, Said has turned to Freud and praised him for 'talking about a composite culture that didn't exclude races and civilisations'.

The world needs Freud's vision. He was a genius for all people, not just the few who occupy his old Vienna home. We must not permit the inspiration of Freud to be denied to any who seek it.

Armed with a mobile

Mobile phones may be irritating, but deadly?

Mobile phones, you know, they make me edgy. For one thing, I never finish half the sentences I start – so many people have my mobile number that I am interrupted almost every time I open my mouth, whether I'm speaking or eating. For another, the microwaves might cause cancer. I always wear an earpiece to avoid frying my brain, but what happens to those waves when the phone is in my pocket? Are they cooking my kidneys? On aeroplanes, there's a nagging awareness that the shifty guy with the DIY haircut two rows forward could be a terrorist. And he may have smuggled a mobile phone aboard.

With all the many other security problems we have now, mobile phones on airliners can be deadly. When oil driller Neil Whitehouse scoffed and sent an 'I love you' text message shortly after takeoff on a British Airways flight from Madrid to Manchester, he received a 12-month jail sentence. The jury heard Whitehouse was within 6 metres of 100 pieces of electronic equipment, with 15 radio systems close by. All were at risk of malfunction from his three little words on the mobile. If a mobile phone could damage a jet, what could a highly-powered microwave weapon do? Some conspiracy theorists believe TWA Flight 800 was accidentally downed in 1996 by a military electro-magnetic ray which was being tested too close to civilian flightpaths. On the other hand, clearly mobile phones can be life savers. No one can forget the desperate calls of alarm from the hijacked American planes, nor the poignant words of farewells and love from the skies.

Military electromagnetic rays and other such weapons are being developed – that's no mere theory. And they are devastating against every kind of electronics, not just in planes. The technology was discovered as a side-effect of atomic bombs – the nuclear blast produced a massive electromagnetic (EM) pulse.

A knockout EM pulse can be built into an ordinary TNT or Semtex stick bomb, the kind favored by terrorists in car bomb attacks. The explosive is cased in aluminium, with a loop of wire at the far end of the stick from the fuse. When the bomb explodes, a wave of electro-magnetic energy is forced up the pipe and into the wire. It discharges like lightning, looking for a conductor to hit – a conductor such as a computer network.

These weapons will be used in terror attacks on financial centres and media stations. The US is already thought to have targeted EM devices against Serbia.

The possibility is that one day, without warning, the computer you rely on will be fried by an EM pulse. In today's dangerous world, just stay positive – this will probably do you less physical harm than using your cell phone.

Yom Kippur and the Hunger Site

I felt like a hypocrite on Yom Kippur. I rose and almost had a glass of water instead of my usual orange juice, a small concession on a day of fast, when you are to neither eat nor drink. I went straight to the exercise machine without slicing and devouring the grapefruit on the marble worktop, and just too look at, I filled the exercise canister with water instead of Isotonic sports fluid.

The water was bottled and refrigerated, and it came from France. Transporters burning hundreds of gallons of diesel had hauled that bottle of water from the Alps to Normandy, and onto a ferry over 22 miles of very ordinary salt water, and across southern England.

For one bottle of water, I paid £2. An aid charity had sent me leaflets pleading for donations, highlighting the life of a southern India boy whose parents died of dysentery. He is seven years old and his village has no clean water. The leaflet said £10 would pay to sink a fresh well and put a pump at its head. For £10, for the price of five bottles of this French mountain water, a village would be free from dysentery.

I sent a donation. But I had also stocked up on bottled water, because I knew Yom Kippur was approaching and I would be trying to fast.

I could have used tap water, of course, but the idea of drinking anything that has been filtered through hundreds of miles of decaying, ancient pipes, made perhaps from lead or some other toxic metal, makes me uncomfortable. I wouldn't eat or drink anything else that had been pumped underground – why make an exception for water?

After pedalling for 30 minutes, I was hungry and thirsty, much more hungry than I might have been if I simply hadn't got round to breakfast yet. There was food in the cupboards, in the freezer, even food growing on the fruit trees around the lawn. If I didn't eat it now, I would eat it later. I was hungry, but I wasn't going hungry, not like I did in Tel Aviv in the early Fifties, when my mother had literally no money for food and my father was sending his wages to some other woman.

The food I didn't eat on Yom Kippur would not be sent to hungry boys from broken families, and the insignificant sum I saved on my weekly food bill would not be building wells in India. I was fasting, but it felt like a poor pretence. I felt like a hypocrite – a hungry hypocrite.

To stop myself from thinking about food and sparkling water, I sat at the computer and logged onto the Web. And did a search for the word 'hunger'.

What came up on screen shocked me. It was several minutes before I was certain that this was not a sick hoax. I had found the Hunger Site, a charity project linked to the United Nations World Food Program.

It offered me the chance to click a button and save someone from death by starvation. Or I could not click the button, and that person would die. My choice.

Above the button a world map flickered. Every few moments one of the countries in the Third World turned grey. The caption below explained the map was based on statistics showing that 24,000 people die from hunger every day. That's 1,000 an hour or one death every 3.6 seconds.

Every time a country went grey, someone starved to death. I sat staring at this gruesome screen for five minutes or more, horrified. About 100 people died. Then I clicked the button marked 'Donate Food' and was taken to a screen stacked with advertisements.

The HungerSite's fact-sheet explains that advertising pays the food bill. Every viewing of the adverts is registered as a 'hit', and for each hit the sponsors each pay half a US cent. With four ads on the page, my hit was worth two cents, or 1.25 pence. That's enough to buy a cup of rice, wheat or maize, which could make the difference for a famine victim on the brink of starvation. Web-users are limited to one click per day.

The UN distributes the donated food, and their spokes-person Abby Spring seems in no doubt of the importance of the site. 'It's great,' she said. 'We're absolutely happy.'

I could not be happy. I could see that, as the HungerSite's reputation spreads and more sponsors are found, a single click could provide several kilos of food. Over a million donations have already been registered, and the HungerSite is 100 per cent profit free – it doesn't make anything at all from its sponsors.

But the pretence of my fast seemed even thinner. I was abstaining from food for a few hours, in a house so glutted with wealth that I didn't even have to raise a finger to save a life. All I had to do with that finger was click a mouse-button. And that kind of wealth is completely normal – everyone in the West has internet access, through colleges and cafés if not their business or home.

Personal computers are being given away in the States by internet service providers, and we too are becoming one of the most wired nations in the world. We can all click and save a life.

Yom Kippur this year made me think more intensely than ever before about world hunger. My fast, as it turned out, was not a futile pretence, but something that achieved great meaning.

Ban the bomb

In a New York strongbox I keep a collection of pistols. One is a traced silver Colt, given to me by the president of Mexico. Others are rare or, in their dark way, beautiful pieces of engineering. I once took pleasure in owning them but, as I saw violence senselessly increasing in the city, I hid them away.

I never look at them, I am not proud of owning them and I am bitterly aware of all the evil that has been done by firearms in private hands. But I cannot bring myself to have them destroyed.

Israel must feel the same way about her nuclear arms.

The government barely admits, of course, to possessing such weapons of mass slaughter. Recently Shimon Peres, the former prime minister, remarked that Israel had 'built a nuclear option not in order to have a Hiroshima but an Oslo'. These non-existent weapons were for peace, not massacre. And that was as near as anyone came to an admission.

But the warheads exist, about 200 of them according to reliable estimates. The world had suspected since the late Sixties, but proof was wanting until 5 October 1986, when the *Sunday Times* published descriptions of the atomic weapons programme from Mordechai Vanunu, a former technician in the bomb factory at Dimona. Vanunu was forcibly transported to Israel, where he is still in prison.

More than three decades ago, following the Six Day War, Menachem Begin and Moshe Dayan learned that the Soviet empire had nuclear missiles trained on Israeli cities. US Secretary of State Henry Kissinger declared that America would not launch into World War III to protect the occupied territories.

A national nuclear power programme was already running – Israel secretly decided to stockpile fully-primed missiles, ready for launch. Seymour Hersh's book *The Samson Option* explains the wholly defensive motivation behind the policy – it was a kind of self-protection-through-suicide, the same desperate thinking that drove Samson to kill the Philistines by tearing down the roof on them – and himself.

The missiles are sited in the Judean foothills, which would probably be the last part of the country to fall to invaders. If Israelis faced utter annihilation, if we had no future but to be 'pushed into the sea', we would tear down the roof of the world.

That deterrent is now a provocation, an excuse for our enemies to taunt and mock us. Saddam Hussein tried to use Israel's nuclear power to pull other Arab countries into his warped worldview. By firing Scuds at Israeli cities, he hoped to provoke a nuclear response.

Atomic missiles could not harm the cowering dictator in his bunker – and he cared nothing for the thousands of Iraqi women and children who would die horribly. If anyone doubts Saddam's callousness, look at his response to the UN

Security Council's tentative olive branch. The world offered to lift sanctions if Iraq could prove, during a 120-day inspection, there were no hidden chemical, nuclear or biowar arsenals.

Saddam sneered at the offer. Sanctions suit him – they keep his people too weak for rebellion.

Nuclear warheads are no deterrent against psychopaths, and they are no defence against monomaniacs. The Afghan-based terrorist Osama bin Laden is widely believed to have obtained at least one portable nuclear bomb, a so-called suitcase device, in a deal for heroin with the Russian mafia. We have to take that capability out of his and Al-Quaida armoury. An atomic blast in Tel Aviv would delight bin Laden's allies, and a forest of nuclear-tipped missiles in Judea could not prevent it.

There is a third disadvantage to our secret programme – it hands excuses to others. India armed herself, hinting that Israel had provided technical support. Pakistan can also demonstrate nuclear capability, claiming that with atomic enemies on either side a nuclear deterrent is essential.

Now the US has opted out of the Comprehensive Test Ban Treaty, giving itself the legal option to start testing the next generation of A-bombs. Congressmen argued that, with the proliferation of nuclear nations, America had to get back in the lab to maintain superiority. When the Pentagon and the World Trade Center towers were hit, there were rumours on the internet that the United States would retaliate with nuclear fire power. 'Nuke them!' was the word.

Israel built those missiles for peace. Now the most useful tactic would be to drop them onto the peace talk table – as bargaining chips. Perhaps finally Israel and the Palestinians will stop killing each other.

We should declare our hand. Half the world has already peeked – Russian and French satellite shots of Israeli silos are said to be so detailed that every leaf on the bushes is visible. So let's come out and say it: Israel has so many missiles, of this and that type, with the destructive power to wipe out this, and this, and this continent.

No one, least of all our enemies, would doubt the heroism of such a gesture. It could set the scene for some long strides towards peace. By bartering away our bombs, Isrsael could make both the Middle East and the whole planet a safer place.

And that, after all, is the purpose for which they were built.

War games

I have been pondering about the damage that hackers can do
to diplomatic relations in the deadlocked Middle East

As I write Palestinian teenagers are showing their anger at
the current political deadlock by taking to the streets with
rocks and petrol bombs. Tragically hundreds have been killed.

Israel has declared cyber warfare illegal, making it unlawful
for hackers to break into Arab sites and festoon them with
Jewish symbols. The law appears ridiculous. Parents should
be delighted when their youngsters respond, not by rioting
but by using their computer expertise to deface web pages.
But in a region desperate for peace, any aggression – even one
in a parallel, virtual world – can have terrifying repercussions.
When the world's diplomats are struggling for solutions,
teens with a talent for hacking are not welcome.

'We need to explain to the Israeli public that we are not a
country of piracy and that children should not be declaring
war,' said Michael Eitan, head of the Government's Internet

Committee. 'We are not talking here about a game but rather about taking risks with the national and international infrastructure.'

He is not exaggerating. Israel has the most computer literate population on the planet, with the highest proportion of PCs to pupils. The Jerusalem Report quoted a hacker identified only as SfromtheSOUTH, who boasted: 'There's no internet service provider in the Arab world that couldn't be knocked out in 15 minutes. In an internet war, the sky would be the limit.'

He added with relish: 'Maybe you can call it the nerd's revenge. The Arabs can blow up buses but nerds can blow up computers.'

Much of the nerd's revenge is puerile – a web gateway based in Jordan was garnished with a picture of Yasser Arafat as a pig, in a situation that would even make a pig blush.

The response of Arab net-users was ferocious. Chain-letter emails went out to sympathisers in Europe and the US, demanding retaliation and calling for an electronic jihad or Holy War.

One claimed: 'The more money the Israelis lose in fixing and strengthening their systems means less money to buy bullets and rockets for use against our children ... maybe you can't hold a gun and fight, but you can contribute to the struggle.'

The idea that a PC in the bedroom becomes a weapon of war is a chilling one. The net is our best hope of improving education globally – to abuse it for warfare is a crime worse than burning books.

Michael Eitan believes: 'The solution to the problem is that there will be an international pact that demands the prosecution of anyone wreaking havoc on the net.' I call on the British Government to seize that lead. The nerd's revenge threatens us all.

11-11 twin towers

Of the many strange outcomes spreading like shockwaves around the world from the destruction of the World Trade Center, few could be more bizarre than the reaction of Karlheinz Stockhausen, the German experimentalist composer.

Stockhausen, who 50 years ago was a star proponent of the 'concrete music' movement in Paris, responded with enthusiasm to the image of 5,000 lives lost under a mountain of concrete: 'What happened there is,' he proclaimed, 'the greatest work of art ever. That characters can bring about in one act what we in music cannot dream of, that people practise madly for 10 years, completely fanatically, for a concert and then die. That is the greatest work of art for the whole cosmos.

'I could not do that. Against that, we composers are nothing.' Herr Stockhausen later claimed that his words were taken out of context. Two of his concerts had to be cancelled in the face of public outcry, and Herr Stockhausen fled the Hamburg music festival, said to be 'greatly upset'.

His reaction is no more extreme, in its own way, than the

grief-fuelled outpouring of fury which has been given voice in America's desire for vengeance. This is a nation which has been loudly anti-war since the Vietnam crisis ended a quarter of a century ago, a country where anti-war films scoop guaranteed Oscars and any foreign policy which could cost a single American life is deemed too dangerous for any president to pursue.

Bill Clinton didn't dare send ground troops in to root out Milosevic and Karadzic. George Bush Snr couldn't set his army rolling down the highway to Baghdad, to drag Saddam Hussein out of his bunker. The risk was too great; men might have been hurt.

But George W. Bush has been handed a blank cheque, on which to write the death toll of as many tens of thousands, even hundreds of thousands, of American troops as it takes to exact justice from the terrorists. And now, as I write, George W. Bush has the awesome responsibility of sending his troops into Afghanistan to eradicate the cancer of terror itself. As Russian veterans of the failed Soviet campaign to invade Afghanistan know, the price of victory in that harsh land of perpetual war could be unbearably high.

The impossible weirdness of all this has been summed up for me by twin revelations about the catastrophe, both of which have been frantically copied around the circles within the internet of those people who, like myself, are fascinated by the paranormal.

One was a rash of translations from Nostradamus, the sixteenth century seer whose cryptic verses appear to foretell much bloodshed and sorrow for the planet around the turn of the Millennium. One verse, which reached me within hours of the televised mass murders, reads: 'In the City of God there will be a great thunder, Two brothers torn apart by Chaos, while the fortress endures, the great leader will succumb, The third big war will begin when the big city is burning.'

I checked this quotation against my electronic file of Nostradamus's predictions, and could find no match. I dismissed it as a hoax. But the truth is stranger, paranormally bizarre: this quatrain was invented several years ago and posted on the internet by a student named Neil Marshall, for his thesis, 'A Critical Analysis of Nostradamus'.

Marshall had wanted to demonstrate how easy it was to ape the seer's style and create sententious, meaningless prophecies. Only this one turned out to have too much, deeply tragic meaning.

The second distorted psychic echo from the explosions took the shape of a number: 11. In fact, two numbers: 11-11. I have written before on the spiritual significance of this pair of numbers, which often seem interwoven into the fabric of turning points in human history.

But these turning points are usually peaceful: the First World War ended at the 11th hour on the 11th day of the 11th month, for instance, and Remembrance Day is still marked on 11 November.

I flew between the twin towers in a small plane nearly 30 years ago with John L. Tishman, the driving force behind the World Trade Center, and I remarked at the time how like a colossal '11' they appeared. They were the tallest structures on the planet then, and I asked John whether they could possibly be vulnerable to a cataclysm, such as an earthquake.

He grinned confidently: 'We built them forever,' he assured me.

I also learned that a presidential limousine was permanently garaged under the North Tower – now, presumably, entombed permanently – and that the Secret Service had several floors.

The tumbling sequence of elevens which spilled out of the horror of 11 September is staggering. If you are of a naturally sceptical turn of mind, I advise you to read no further.

After 11 September there are 111 days to the end of the year, since this was the 254th day of 2001 (2 + 5 + 4 = 11). The first plane to hit the towers was Flight 11 by American Airlines (A is the first letter of the alphabet, so AA = 11). New York City has 11 letters and New York State was the 11th state to be added to the union.

There were 110 stories in each tower (11 x 10 = 110, multiplied by two ... 11-11 for the twin towers). The code for New York is 1001 and the US emergency code is 911. The date of the attack 9/11 (9 + 1 + 1 = 11).

These names have 11 letters: Afghanistan, The Pentagon, George W Bush, Air Force One, Bill Clinton, Saudi Arabia. Remembrance Day is on 11 November and Jesus Christ has eleven letters.

Strange. Upsetting. Inexplicable.

Blowback

As I turned on my PC to write, I checked my website and found it had been . . . taken over. I would have said 'hijacked' but that word, like many which my mind regarded as neutral – like skyscraper, rubble, tower, pilot – is now steeped in bitterness.

Someone with the wit to hack an internet server but without the intelligence to write cogently or think coherently had dumped a rambling to-whom-it-may-concern letter on the front page of my site at www.urigeller.com

It was signed 'Philo Bunny' which gave me no clue to the culprit. I suspect the author may have been Jewish, if only because Palestine was spelled 'Palestein'. This rant against Israel, Arabs and the US was headed 'We're coming to get you' – although I hoped this referred to America's vow to hunt down Osama bin Laden, I was uneasy that it might refer to me.

It is not necessary to be well known to be the target of racist abuse or worse. In the US two men were murdered in sickening 'reprisals' by white Americans: one was a Muslim, the other a Sikh. The Sikh's family told police they had been subjected to taunts and threats since 11 September because their turbans and beards gave them a likeness to bin Laden.

Bin Laden, of course, is not a Sikh – nor is he a Muslim worthy of the name. I know the vast majority of Muslims will agree with me.

The advantage of being well known, when racist abuse occurs, is that the police will take the threats seriously. An officer interviewed me, offered advice on security, and logged the incident.

A few hours later, walking along London's High Holborn, I saw the windows of the Arab Press building had been smashed. The damage was at head height, as if thugs had come equipped with hammers for the task.

In the aftermath of the attacks, there is a palpable atmosphere of dread and violence. Some of it is ugly and frightening – every Jew recognises the evil resonance of windows shattered with hammers, an act of intimidation inevitably recalling the Kristallnacht of November 1938, when Nazi militia attacked Jewish homes, businesses and synagogues across Germany and Austria.

But some of the crackling, foreboding atmospherics are different. There were no anonymous hackers spreading intimidation in the Thirties, no gung-ho news groups, no calls to genocide circulated by email, no messages flashed between terrorist cells by mobile.

The mobile phones which gave doomed passengers on board four hijacked American Airlines planes a chance to say their heart-breaking goodbyes were no different from the pay-as-you-go phones, bought one day and discarded the next, by which their killers had kept in touch.

The technology which the West has developed for society and for global capitalism is now being used to destroy society and tear down capitalism around the world – just as the idiosyncratic website I nurture to bring a seedling of peace to the internet has been trampled by a cyber-terrorist who wants to see the world at war.

In intelligence jargon, this is 'blowback' – the unforeseen consequences of any policy. It was probably coined by a military agent who had seen the horrific damage that the wrong end of a bazooka can cause – stand behind a WWII anti-tank bazooka as the missile blasts out, and the blowback of searing gases will strip the skin from your face.

But the word also recalls a verse from the Book of Prophets (Hosea, 8:7) – 'They sow wind, and they shall reap whirlwind.' What blows back can be more horrific than any carnage caused by the weapon.

American foreign policy has provoked genocidal blowback before now. In his book: *Blowback, The Costs and Consequences of American Empire*, Chalmers Johnson writes:

'In pursuing the war in Vietnam in the early 1970s, President Richard Nixon and his national security adviser Henry Kissinger ordered more bombs dropped on rural Cambodia than had been dropped on Japan during all of World War II, killing at least three-quarters of a million Cambodian peasants and helping legitimize the murderous Khmer Rouge movement under Pol Pot. In his subsequent pursuit of revenge and ideological purity Pol Pot ensured that another million and a half Cambodians, this time mainly urban dwellers, were murdered.'

If the key to blowback is that it turns our society's best facets against us, we begin to see why Palestinian suicide bombers choose discos and pizzerias as the scenes of their carnage. Just as the hijackers on 11 September could have piloted their flying bombs into nuclear power stations to cause maximum devastation, or targeted military mini-cities such as West Point academy, 50 miles north of New York, so the Palestinians could have slaughtered soldiers or politicians. But the military is not the target any more.

I am approached by religious fanatics occasionally. They usually claim that my parascientific abilities, or sometimes my Jewishness, are the gift of the devil. I have never met any fundamentalist, Jewish, Muslim, Christian or of any other faith, who knew the first thing about the religion he or she professed. Their perverted mindset is usually based on a few sacred quotations ripped out of context by some tin guru and scrawled on the back of a cigarette packet.

Nothing else can explain the eagerness to commit suicide by people who call themselves Muslims. As a New York imam explained on CNN suicide is prohibited under Islam.

The punishment? To repeat that awful death, endlessly, throughout eternity.

That's real blowback.